The First Forensic Hanging

The First Forensic Hanging

The Toxic Truth that Killed Mary Blandy

by
Summer Strevens

PEN & SWORD **HISTORY**

AN IMPRINT OF PEN & SWORD BOOKS LTD.
YORKSHIRE – PHILADELPHIA

First published in Great Britain in 2018 by
Pen & Sword History
An imprint of
Pen & Sword Books Ltd
Yorkshire - Philadelphia

ISBN 978 1 52673 618 5

A CIP catalogue record for this book is
available from the British Library.

Printed and bound in England
By TJ International Ltd.

Pen & Sword Books Ltd incorporates the Imprints of Pen & Sword Books Archaeology, Atlas,
Aviation, Battleground, Discovery, Family History, History, Maritime, Military, Naval, Politics,
Railways, Select, Transport, True Crime, Fiction, Frontline Books, Leo Cooper, Praetorian
Press, Seaforth Publishing, Wharncliffe and White Owl.

For a complete list of Pen & Sword titles please contact

PEN & SWORD BOOKS LIMITED
47 Church Street, Barnsley, South Yorkshire, S70 2AS, England
E-mail: enquiries@pen-and-sword.co.uk
Website: www.pen-and-sword.co.uk
or
PEN AND SWORD BOOKS
1950 Lawrence Rd, Havertown, PA 19083, USA
E-mail: Uspen-and-sword@casematepublishers.com
Website: www.penandswordbooks.com

Contents

Acknowledgements

While Mary Blandy has been the subject of several dedicated biographies, not to mention her appearance in any number of collective works concerning 'distinguished victims of the scaffold', her story was also the inspiration for Joan Morgan's *The Hanging Wood*, adapted for the stage in the late 1960's, and adapted again by the BBC in 1980 for the *A Question of Guilt* series. Indeed, it is the question of Mary's guilt which keeps her story alive and divides opinion to this day. Yet in writing this book, as well as primarily addressing the doubts concerning the verdict handed down to Mary nearly 270 years ago – the judgement resting on the matter of her 'intention' in the poisoning of her father and the extent to which her coercive lover, Captain William Cranstoun, was responsible for this murder by proxy – I have also sought to bring into focus the part played by Dr Anthony Addington, and the consequent 'forensic legacy' borne of his involvement with the case.

In his *Science and the Criminal*, published in 1911, the chemist and forensic scientist Ainsworth Mitchell made note of the fact that Mary Blandy's case was 'remarkable as being the first one of which there is any detailed record, in which convincing scientific proof of poisoning was given'. Indeed, this was the first time detailed medical evidence had been presented in court on a charge of murder by poisoning, and consequently the first time a conviction was secured on the basis of such evidence. While the considerable public attention garnered by Addington's appearing as the principal and expert for the prosecution was to make the doctor's career, his testimony was also pivotal in paving the way for the advancement in, and later acceptance of scientific testing in a court of law, and the contribution of modern forensic understanding crucial to the veracity of the justice served in courtrooms today. Allowing for an acknowledgement falling outside of the literary sphere, primary recognition is necessarily granted to Dr Addington.

Of course, I am also most grateful to all those others who have assisted in the research and writing of this book, not least to Victor Bingham whose own insights into Mary Blandy's case are extensive. I would also like to acknowledge Katherine Watson, senior lecturer in the History of Medicine at Oxford Brookes University, her published research concerning the intersection of medicine, crime and the law proving invaluable.

Grateful thanks are also due to Father Martyn Griffiths, Rector of St Mary the Virgin, Henley-on-Thames, where Mary was baptised, and buried, for his assistance in accessing the church's historic registers, and to Justin Hawkins, Head of Communication for the Criminal Cases Review Commission, for clarifying the position with regards to Mary obtaining a posthumous pardon. I would also like to extend my grateful thanks to Phil Simms, News Editor of the Henley Standard, to Philip Bell for the use of his superb photography, and to Lolly Green, licensee of The Little Angel, Remenham. I am further indebted to David Eggleton, the organiser of *Henley Ghost Tours*, an authority on Mary from the paranormal perspective; certainly, she still makes her presence felt in her hometown, and is neither gone nor forgotten!

I must also extend my gratitude to my publishers, Pen & Sword, to my commissioning editor, Heather Williams, and make special mention of the forbearance of my copy editor, Carol Trow; any mistakes are mine, not hers. As ever, I am indebted to my partner, Jack Gritton, who continues to respond to my cries for help in the face of my inadequate IT capabilities, still found to be considerably wanting!

To all those aforementioned, and everyone else who has given their time, and guided and shared their knowledge and insights, and shown an encouraging interest when I myself have plumbed the depths of self-doubt, a very big thank you.

Summer Strevens

2018

Author's Notes

In view of the inordinately lengthy title, '*Miss Mary Blandy's own account of the affair between her and Mr. Cranstoun, from the commencement of their acquaintance in the year 1746 to the death of her father in August, 1751, with all the circumstances leading to that unhappy event*' for the ease of the reader (and that of the author!) the title of this publication will be abbreviated to Mary Blandy's '*Own Account*' throughout.

Contemporary monetary values have been calculated using *MeasuringWorth.com*, a very useful website estimating the purchasing power of sterling from 1270 to the present day.

William Roughead, the well-known Scottish lawyer and amateur criminologist who was an early proponent of the modern 'true crime' literary genre, states in his *Trial of Mary Blandy*, published in 1914, that Mary's mother's name was also Mary, however transcripts of the registers for Henley Parish Church confirm that her name was in fact 'Anne' (also appearing as 'Ann').

Introduction

'For the sake of decency, gentlemen, don't hang me high.' This was the last request of modest murderess Mary Blandy, who was hanged for the poisoning of her father in 1752. Concerned that the young men amongst the crowd who had thronged to see her execution might look up her skirts as she was 'turned off' by the hangman, this last nod to propriety might appear farcical in one who was about to meet her maker. Yet this was just another aspect of a case which attracted so much public attention in its day that some determined spectators even went to the lengths of climbing through the courtroom windows to get a glimpse of Mary while on trial. Indeed, her case remained newsworthy for the best part of 1752, for months garnering endless scrutiny and a mixed reaction in the press, as well as spawning a plethora of publications and pamphlets, claiming to be the 'genuine account' and the 'genuine letters' of Mary Blandy, some of which maintained her innocence, as indeed she did herself to the very last.

Yet Mary Blandy's trial, which began at 8am on 3rd March 1752, and lasted until 9 o'clock that evening (the jury returning a guilty verdict after only five minutes deliberation) was also notable in that it was the first time that detailed medical evidence had been presented in a court of law on a charge of murder by poisoning, and the first time that any court had accepted toxicological evidence in an arsenic poisoning case.

Of abiding interest to historians of forensic medicine, the topic of poisoning itself has long tended to attract the greatest attention, and indeed often confrontation with regards to criminal proceedings, when the principles of medical science have met those of law and justice; it has been posited that murder cases involving poisoning are the most difficult of all in which to secure a conviction.

While at the time of Mary's trial the field of forensic toxicology was still in its relative infancy, the history of forensics itself can be traced as far back as Ancient Rome (in Latin the word *forensic* means 'in open court') as it was the Roman attorney Quintilian who was first to employ forensics in the defence of a blind man accused of murdering his mother. Thanks to the evidence of a bloody palm print found at the scene, Quintilian's client was acquitted. Of course, the science has come along way since then, the massive advancements in autopsy procedures and toxicological tests are a given; with the benefits of toxicological screening in authenticating proof of suspected poisoning, today's pathologist is able to evaluate the cause or contribution of a poison to a victim's death. Yet prior to this, it was the role played by medical men in the legal process, representing historical trends in the acceptance of professional authority in the judicial arena, that are necessarily of interest. And with regards to the enhanced status and authority of forensic evidence presented at a criminal trial today, it is Dr Anthony Addington who must be singled out as being of seminal importance.

Of course, the forensic evidence presented by Addington at Mary Blandy's trial would be regarded as rudimentary by today's standards and in no way definitive. Yet the forensic legacy of the acceptance of Addington's application of chemistry to a criminal investigation is nevertheless crucial. Proving the presence of a poison formerly considered undetectable marks Mary Blandy's case as a milestone in forensic and judicial history. Once scientific testing became accepted by courts, chemists began advancing and applying many other processes to methods of identifying evidence in poisoning cases and linking it to a suspect. The days of arsenic as the 'perfect poison' were numbered.

Appearing as an expert witness for the prosecution, Dr Addington was unable to analyse Francis Blandy's organs for traces of arsenic, because the technology did not exist at the time. His evidence was nevertheless persuasive and he was able to convince the court on the basis of his tests that the powder Mary had mixed into her father's food and drink was indeed arsenic. Notwithstanding Addington's findings, it was the matter of Mary's guilt based on her supposed 'intention' to poison her father that was the crux of her case however, though her lover, would-be bigamist William Henry Cranstoun, was doubtless complicit in her crime. Commonly held as the instigator of the proxy murder of Francis Blandy by Mary's hand, of course, Cranstoun never stood trial, derided for abandoning Mary to face her fate, and the gallows, alone.

To all appearances, the Honourable Captain William Henry Cranstoun, an army officer and the son of a Scottish nobleman, seemed an eminently eligible match, especially in the eyes of Mary's socially pretentious parents who were bent on securing a suitable husband for their daughter. While the Blandys were well aware that Cranstoun's financial situation was less than satisfactory, they were nevertheless beguiled by the prospect of an aristocratic match for Mary, unaware that Cranstoun was an exploitative opportunist of the first order. And while Mary's complexion bore the scars of a bout of smallpox contracted in childhood, she was nevertheless still regarded as something of a 'catch', and indeed 'her powers of attraction were enhanced by the rumour of her fortune' which local gossip placed in the region of ten thousand pounds. As would later become apparent, the speculative sum was considerably inflated, but in the interest of self-aggrandisement, Francis Blandy said nothing to refute this wealthy assumption. Besides, people have murdered for far less.

Cranstoun's plans were upset however on the exposure of his earlier marriage to a wife still alive and well in Scotland. Though he disputed the validity of his prior union, while Mary might have been completely taken in by him, her father began to see Cranstoun for the man he really was. With the hostility of his prospective father-in-law a decided obstacle to his getting his hands on Mary's sizeable dowry, the old man had to go. Affording himself of the advantage of long-distance poisoning by proxy, Mary was manipulated into the murder of her own father, the instrument of his destruction, and ultimately her own.

It has been questioned how a woman of Mary's education and maturity could have been so taken in. Locally respected as a well-mannered and well-educated young woman, she was in her late twenties when she first met Cranstoun. In hindsight, she may have done well to heed the words of the *Newgate Calendar* – that supposedly moralising publication devoured by a past readership hungry for the details of those who had fallen from virtue to vice:

> 'Young ladies should be cautious of listening to the insidious address
> of artful love as they know not how soon, and how unsuspectedly,
> their hearts may be engaged to their own destruction'.

Whether or not the lovelorn Miss Blandy emphatically believed that the powders supplied by Cranstoun were indeed an ancient 'love philtre', harmless in nature, yet guaranteed to engender her father's approval of the man she loved, they were, of course, arsenic. Though Mary never denied having administered the poison, she was insistent throughout her trial, and until the moment the noose was placed around her neck, that the powders 'had been given me with another intent'. Persuaded by Cranstoun that her father would suffer no deleterious side-effects, Mary was adamant in her belief that the substance which she stirred into her father's tea and gruel, at Cranstoun's direction, was nothing more injurious than an innocuous powdered preparation intended to improve her father's opinion of the Captain. In all likelihood, the powders which Cranstoun alleged he had sourced from a Scottish 'mystic' had been purchased for a few pennies over the counter of an apothecary shop.

Though Mary's legal counsel put up a vigorous defence, she herself making an impassioned speech extolling her innocence, needless to say, the jury did not believe her, and in spite of Cranstoun's clear involvement, that his actions did not mitigate her own. In addition to the forensic evidence presented, the decidedly detrimental witness testimony and the circumstantial evidence put forward by the prosecution also weighed heavy; notably that of the Blandy household servants who testified that they had seen Mary tampering with her father's food and that she had later tried to destroy downright incriminating evidence. The fact that two of those servants suffered violent illness after consuming left-overs from Francis Blandy's table also did nothing to support Mary's protested probity.

One has to question whether it was possible that Mary was so much in Cranstoun's thrall that she rationalised away these warning signs, most notably the deterioration in her own father's health. In modern parlance, was she at the back of the queue when common sense was being handed out? Yet if we are to believe Mary's own assertions, in the pithy words of one of her later commentators, 'Mary Blandy died for love. The tragedy of it was, she died on the gallows.'

As a footnote to her death, the ignominy that Mary feared at her execution, occasioning the quote opening this introduction, was to be posthumously founded; the provision of a coffin having been overlooked, after being cut down from the gallows, when Mary's body was unceremoniously slung over the shoulder of an official, her legs were exposed to the gawping multitude who had gathered to watch her hang.

Nearly 270 years after her death, the debate about whether or not Mary Blandy unwittingly murdered her father, her moral culpability and indeed the matter of her 'intention' in the case is still a lively one; doubts expressed concerning the guilty verdict have even prompted an application to the Criminal Cases Review Commission with a view to overturning this contentious conviction and obtaining a posthumous pardon for Mary. Certainly, for his part, had Cranstoun stood trial alongside Mary, then he would doubtless have weighed heavily in the scales of Lady Justice, but as soon as he got wind of Mary's likely arrest, he deserted overseas, saving his own neck. Past and present detractors of Cranstoun have, however, taken comfort from the fact that the 'profligate wretch' who was 'a disgrace to the noble blood from which he derived existence' himself died painfully, and in timely retribution a little less than eight months after Mary's execution, and while his death was attributed to natural causes, his agonies were such that at the end he suffered much as Francis Blandy had.

However posterity might view the extent of Mary Blandy's involvement and guilt, regardless of the forensic evidence presented, it is difficult to ignore the contemporary opinions, though coloured by the judgement of another age, which determined the final verdict. The matter remains open to question, and the possible contemporary outcome of Mary's trial being brought as a 'cold case' in a court of law today is discussed in the last chapter. Certainly, Mary's father was forgiving of his 'Poor love-sick girl', though on his deathbed Francis Blandy may have rued the consequences of exaggerating his daughter's dowry, the incentive for Cranstoun's greed, and in turn the catalyst for his own demise and that of his daughter. In his last hours, in mitigation for Mary's actions, Francis Blandy was heard to exclaim 'What won't a girl do for a man she loves?'

In Mary Blandy's case, did that amount to murder?

Chapter 1

'A son is a son 'til he gets a wife, but a daughter is a daughter all her life.'

I f we are to subscribe to the kitsch notion that 'nice girls don't', and in this instance do not murder their fathers (or anyone else for that matter!) then Mary Blandy presents herself as something of a enigma. From a respectable, middle–class background, raised with all the advantages that her comfortable situation could offer, Mary was the only child of Francis Blandy, a prosperous lawyer and the Town Clerk of Henley-on-Thames in Oxfordshire and his wife Anne, the former Miss Stevens of Culham Court, a lady described as 'an emblem of chastity and virtue'. Married in Henley's parish church of St Mary the Virgin on 22 September 1719, Anne was the daughter of Thomas Stevens, a gentleman of Henley; Francis himself hailing from an old Berkshire family, the Blandys of Letcombe Bassett, in the Vale of the White Horse, some thirty miles distant from where he had set up his successful business.

While we know that Mary was born into a relatively privileged station in life; with a large client base, Francis was doing well for himself, and was noted as a person of some importance in the county, the exact date of her birth is not known. However, the records for baptisms celebrated in Henley's parish church for the year 1720 show that 'Mary, of Fransis [sic] ' was christened on 15 July. As English parish registers, as a general rule, recorded dates of baptisms rather than births, and, as the average age at baptism increased from one week old in the middle of the seventeenth century to one month by the middle of the nineteenth century, it would be fair to assume that Mary was 31 years old when she ascended the makeshift gallows erected in the Castle Yard in Oxford on 6 April 1752.

In the year of Mary's birth, while naturally, the arrival of their daughter would have taken centre stage for Francis and Anne, other more worldly events worthy of note were taking place. Six years into the reign of King George I, the first of the Hanoverian monarchs, Britain, along with Spain, France, Austria and the Dutch Republic signed the Treaty of The Hague, effectively ending the War of the Quadruple Alliance. 1720 also saw feverish speculation in the shares of the South Sea Company, one of the largest stock scams of all time, the sudden collapse of investment resulting in the financial crash which burst the 'South Sea Bubble' with thousands losing their life savings. This was also the year in which the infamous cross-dressing Anne Bonny and Mary Read were found guilty of pirating, and sentenced to death in Spanish Town, Jamaica, only to discover that there were advantages to their sex after all when both won a stay of execution after 'pleading their belly' – that is to say they were pregnant. Caribbean pirate 'Calico Jack' Rackham fared less well, however. Captured by the Royal Navy, he was hanged at Port Royal. Global issues aside, on a domestic note, and possibly appealing to Mrs Blandy and other devotees of culinary advances, this was also the year in which Mrs Clements successfully marketed the first paste-style mustard – her product even tickled the palate of the king himself, whose liking for the mustard assured Mrs Clements' success, as well as numerous orders from those keen followers of royal tastes. As we shall see, Mary's parents were of a particularly snobbish bent, and may well have enjoyed liberal helpings of this new-fangled, royally endorsed condiment.

As their only child, Mary was 'brought up with great and rare tenderness'. Judging from the approximation of Mary's date of birth, taking into account the slight baptismal delay, the 19-year-old Anne Blandy must have conceived in a timely fashion after the couple's wedding, yet the absence of any later children might be attributed to some obstetric difficulty she experienced when giving birth, as alluded to in a later chapter when Mary raised the matter relative to her mother's last illness. Their precious and beloved daughter was doubtless spoiled by her doting parents, growing up in the Blandy's mansion in Hart Street, surrounded by lovely gardens, close to the bridge over the Thames; the street, formerly known as High Street, ran from Henley Bridge into what is now Market Place. Said to have been an intelligent child and fond of reading, Mary was educated at home by her mother, herself described as 'in mind elevated'. Though women from even prosperous backgrounds received an inferior education to those of their male counterparts, Mary must have been a bright girl, as by the age of fourteen she was noted as having reached a standard 'which others of like station and opportunities rarely achieve until they are twenty'. In addition to schooling her daughter to a level of feminine literacy deemed adequate for the times, Anne Blandy's instruction also encompassed 'the principles of religion and piety, according to the rites and ceremonies of the Church of England.' Later admonishers of Mary's character were hasty to point out that clearly her mother's admirable qualities had not been inherited by her daughter, never mind the pious principles she had striven to instil. Notwithstanding Mary's academic aptitude, we can assume that as well as a proficiency in music, drawing and possibly languages, dancing was added to the social graces which would mark her out as eminently acceptable in polite society, and to that end a dancing master would have been engaged by her parents to add a polish to their daughter's social 'finish'. Not only would such instruction be a prelude to the ballroom, Mary would also benefit from the additional refinements such tuition offered, in etiquette, deportment and the cultivation of that air of relaxed assurance so much admired in the age. A credit to her socially aspiring parents, such accomplishments were also a necessary preparation for contracting a prestigious marriage; Francis Blandy after all sought only the best for his daughter, and his 'whole Thoughts were bent to settle her advantageously in the World'.

Desirable social accomplishments aside, Mary must nevertheless have been acutely aware of her pockmarked complexion, a lasting reminder of the bout of smallpox she had contracted in childhood. In the eighteenth century, smallpox in Britain was at its height – no respecter of rank, affecting all levels of society, this disease of 'princes and paupers' was responsible for 400,000 deaths annually in Europe, and of those lucky enough to survive, most were left with disfiguring scars. Though the physical ravages of the disease were commonly described as rendering 'the eyes and cheeks of the betrothed maiden the objects of horror to the lover', Mary was still regarded as a very desirable matrimonial prospect, not lessened by the considerable dowry which Francis was offering along with his daughter's hand.

At the time, as well as Francis's finances, the fortunes of Henley itself were also flourishing. A genteel town, the name of Henley-on-Thames retains a certain cachet today, as host to the annual Henley Royal Regatta. Set against the Chiltern landscape of wooded hills and green fields, prosperity was guaranteed thanks to continuing river trade and the increase in stagecoach traffic. From the late seventeenth century, the town's advantageous position on important routes to and from London turned it into a major coaching centre, which in turn had a significant impact on Henley's social tone and infrastructure. This mode of transport, though not particularly quick or comfortable, made it feasible for surrounding country gentry to attend the newly fashionable round of assemblies, balls and social seasons, with the added advantage that the smartest elements of society brought incidental trade to the town. This in turn prompted an increase in the range of local commercial ventures, reflected in the growth of the number of businesses meeting the demand from a wealthier clientele, be they transient travellers or fashionable customers from the town's local élite. As one would expect, as a staging post on the coaching route to and from London, not to mention the turnpike through Henley linking with roads to the fashionable spa resort of Bath, the town also offered a choice of well-established inns. One, the White Hart, which gave its name to the street on which the Blandy's house stood, operated a six-horse service to the capital three times a week. Catering to these new and increasing patterns of consumption, along with the everyday high street staples provided by the grocer's shop, linen drapers and ironmongers, new specialist retailers also appeared, such as brandy merchants, booksellers and even a watchmaker. Before long the wig-makers, milliners and purveyors of other luxuries items set up business, alongside the ubiquitous pawnbroker of course – this was after all the age of credit. The rise of consumerism in the eighteenth century saw the emergence of the concept of imaginary money, or 'credit', and then as now the materialistic desires of some were greater than the depths of their pockets.

Despite the fashionable delights and distractions which London and Bath offered, Henley itself was fast becoming the focus of a varied, albeit provincial social scene of its own, involving local landowners, clergymen, leading merchants, the ranking officers of regionally based militia as well as professionals, like Mary's father.

One might form the impression that while Francis was well regarded in his field, prospering as a lawyer as well as holding the position of Henley's Town Clerk, he was nonetheless still one of those middle-class professionals (though at the higher end of the spectrum) who sought to bolster his position in society; though he was of an old, respected Berkshire family, it never did any harm to aspire to a higher rung on the social ladder. Though he was renowned for his grudging frugality, and an avaricious nature, Mary's father nevertheless allowed for one exception, and was noted for his ostentatious hospitality. His table 'whether filled with company or not, was every day plenteously supplied'; money well spent in Francis's view, in a show of personal fortune and an exercise in self-aggrandisement. Certainly, social status was paramount as the distinguishing feature of early-modern English society. Social hierarchy determined everything about a person and was instrumental in shaping their entire lives. Yet in the seventeenth and eighteenth centuries, though the aristocracy had been the most powerful section of the British elite, increasingly wealth became a determining influence on social rank. What better way then, for a provincial solicitor to heighten his social standing, and ensure an estimable marriage for Mary than to boast of his affluence, reflected in the significant amount he was offering for his daughter's dowry. For a man in his professional position, Francis Blandy would have had many opportunities of mingling with his 'betters', and when they learned of the £10,000 which the Henley attorney had amassed, for 'such was the figure at which public opinion put it' he may even have been treated as their near equal. Yet, as would later become apparent, the assumed wealth which he had vaunted was considerably exaggerated, and the sum he was offering as Mary's dowry was in fact far less than he made it out to be. Though he could not have foreseen it, that Francis said nothing to refute these wealthy assumptions would ultimately be to his detriment; 'What was intended for her [Mary's] Promotion proved his Death and her Destruction.' The consequences of his ambition lay in the future, however; the hunt for a suitable husband for Mary was now on.

As the local pool of eligible suitors in the environs of Henley seemed distinctly shallow, the Blandys decamped to Bath for the season, which was then acknowledged as the great matrimonial marketplace. Bath was certainly the place to be. With the city's growth, Bath had emerged as a centre of pleasure and Georgian elegance, a chic destination rivalling even London as the place to be seen. Thackray certainly thought so, writing:

> 'As for Bath, all history went and bathed and drank there. George II and his Queen, Prince Frederick and his Court, scarce a charac-ter one can mention of the early last century but was seen in that famous Pump Room, where Beau Nash presided, and his picture hung between the busts of Newton and Pope.'

During the 'season', which ran from October to June, at least two balls a week were held, in addition to a range of concerts and other events. Beyond the splendid new facades of grandiose public buildings such as the Pump Room and the Assembly Rooms, which formed the hub of fashionable Georgian society in the city, described as 'the most noble and elegant of any in the kingdom', the opulent interiors buzzed with the conversation of fashionable visitors; those who came to bathe, to drink the famous waters, gamble, eat, drink and dance, as well as those bent on brokering a propitious marriage.

Yet the social mix comprised of all sorts, from aristocrats to the aspiring merchant classes, affording the opportunity for the single daughters of ambitious provincials to rub shoulders with noble company. And notwithstanding having 'suffered the indignity of the smallpox' Mary was obviously an attractive young woman, described as having a fine figure, 'her brilliant black eyes and abundant hair' apparently 'redeemed a face otherwise rather ordinary' – this particular commentator was apparently gracious enough to refrain from any allusion to Mary's evident facial scarring, that 'stole the bloom from the cheeks of many a sparkling belle'. In spite of her father's miserly nature, though Francis Blandy may have grumbled about the considerable outlay necessary for travel, accommodation and the cost of the season's entertainments, it would also have been essential for his daughter to be properly attired. As the basis for the visit to Bath was to secure a suitable son-in-law, Mary being fashionably and expensively dressed was a given; a necessary expenditure which, in addition to the 'pleasures so expensive', must have been written-off by Francis Blandy as a 'business cost'. Rather a harsh view but in the eighteenth century finding a husband was regarded as a business, the institution of marriage viewed as a means of gaining advancement; marrying for money, power or position were accepted conventions, and the considerations of securing a financially and socially acceptable bridegroom outweighed any notions of romance, or even compatibility for that matter. Certainly, there were no guarantees of a 'fairy tale' ending; once a young lady came out in society, she had but one duty to fulfil; to make a suitable match.

Although Francis himself was noted as appearing 'genteel in dress', the Blandy account at the dressmakers must have been sizeable, as no doubt Mrs Blandy would have availed herself of the opportunity of acquiring some new dresses of her own - who wouldn't in the circumstances! In the 1730's the 'sack back' dress which had become increasingly fashionable, and would remain so until the 1780's, required a considerable amount of costly fabric. The styling of the gown called for five or six panels of silk, folded and stitched into two box pleats at the centre back of the dress which fell loose from the shoulder to the floor with a slight train. As the dress flowed down it was incorporated into the fullness of the skirt, worn over a matching petticoat, beneath which was another hooped petticoat. These petticoats, usually made of linen with split cane hoops stitched in at intervals were to reach their widest proportions in the 1740s and 1750s and at their zenith measured over five feet across. As with many such fashions, it is hard to say why such cumbersome outfits were popular, however with such excesses reserved for formal occasions, it may have been that such gowns, displaying an excess of richly embroidered cloth, were an opulent and ostentatious indicator of the wearer's wealth (or in Mary's case, that of her father).

Fashionably attired then, laced, ruffled and ribboned from head to toe, in order to protect Mary's new embroidered silk brocade slippers from the unavoidable dirt and filth of Bath's streets, if the Blandys had not engaged a carriage, then a 'chair' was a must. Conveyance in a sedan chair would have cost in the region of sixpence for half a mile before ten in the evening, after ten o'clock rising to a shilling, provided that a passenger did not order the chairman to stop, perhaps to gossip with a friend, the 'meter' frozen, so to speak, unless the halt exceeded ten minutes. We can imagine Francis carping about these costs as well. After depositing their passengers in the grand porticos of Bath's Assembly Rooms or perhaps the Pump Room, chairmen would wait out the gathering for the homeward fares in the basement below, where their recent earnings were often staked at dice or cards. There was plenty of gambling going on above stairs too – those not disposed to the tread of the dancefloor preferring instead to play for high stakes at Hazard or Piquet. Other popular card games included Faro, Whist, Vingt-et-un – better known today as 'Twenty-One' or 'Blackjack' – and the higher-class Baccarat, played with dice; the loss of an entire family estate at the gaming table was not unknown at this time. Indeed, it would seem that gambling, in virtually any form, was a Georgian obsession; in fact, it was often referred to as the English Vice. It was not unknown for a high stakes wager to be placed on two raindrops running down a windowpane of White's – the London gentlemen's club famous for its betting-book facilitating wagers on literally anything – odds were even placed on the number of cats that would walk down opposite sides of the street. Yet it was members of Brooks's, another gentlemen's club, who callously wagered on the life of a man who apparently fell down dead on the street outside – the suggestion that someone should go and see if he could be revived regarded as very poor form since it might affect the outcome of the bet... Though it seemed most endemic and excessive in the upper classes, gambling on games of chance was in no way exclusive to that set, the lower classes as adept at losing money as their social superiors. While the appeal was apparently universal, one would assume, however, that the parsimonious Francis Blandy would have refrained from any such pernicious pecuniary pursuits.

In addition to her physical attractions, and we must assume her costly dress, Mary was also noted for her wit, vivacity and good nature, and apparently threw herself enthusiastically into all the gaieties that Bath's season had to offer. With her winning ways Mary was to prove herself an 'immediate social success'; she even enjoyed the prestigious honour of dancing with royalty, taking a turn with Frederick, Prince of Wales. We can imagine then, while Mrs Blandy must have been puffed up with pride at her daughter being marked out for such singular regal favour, from the side-lines Francis remained keenly alert to the opportunity of a useful introduction on the back of this mark of royal preference, and to the prospect of his daughter catching the eye of an eligible beau. Any approach would have to be made in accordance with rigid social etiquette, however. In this respect men were expected to be extremely active in the ballroom to make up for the passivity required of the chaperoned ladies present. Protocol dictated demure hesitation on the peripheries, until a gentleman came to speak to them, convey them to the refreshments, or asked them to dance. The taboo of crossing the dancefloor unescorted, never mind being forward enough to ask a gentleman to dance would have been viewed as unseemly in the extreme, and amounting to social suicide. With the dictates of social niceties strictly observed, while opportunity might have allowed for some coquettish eye contact and use of the fan, young ladies would still have been kept at a safe arm's length, the touch of a gloved hand being the only physicality deemed decently appropriate. Though the country dances popular at less exalted gatherings afforded a greater opportunity for hand holding, it would be the early 1800s before the 'shockingly intimate' Waltz was introduced to English ballrooms, initially denounced as vulgar and immoral. Princess Victoria, in an early diary of 1832, wrote 'Mama has allowed the Waltz to be played,' in tones of mingled delight and excitement.

Indeed, candidates for Mary's gloved hand were not lacking. However, in the eyes of her parents, it was imperative that any such suitor was in a confirmed position to be able to offer a proposal of marriage that was advantageous to their daughter, namely a high-ranking station in life, and an income to match. Needless to say, the approaches of an enthusiastic young apothecary were immediately evaluated as unworthy by Mary's socially astute father, as were those of two further keen suitors, who, though appealing enough to Mary, were deemed 'too limited' to entertain any real hope. The next to profess his affections however initially seemed to tick all the right boxes. He was a captain in the army – known in all records as merely 'Captain D.' – though he was of no great fortune, he gave the prospect of a son-in-law who held the king's commission which appealed to Francis's vanity. Besides which, connections in military circles would look well in the ranks of Henley's high society. Opportunity was swiftly acted upon, and the couple became engaged. But alas, Mary's much hoped-for march toward the altar, like the walks she enjoyed with her fiancé through the fields around her Henley home were rudely cut short, her plans for marriage derailed when the eligible captain received orders to join his regiment on active service abroad.

Her hopes of love and matrimony dashed, while Mary was now in her mid-twenties though it was a less than desirable situation; there was still time to find a husband, though if she remained a spinster for very much longer, she ran the risk of 'being left on the shelf'. Hours filled with the genteel distractions of reading, letter-writing and needlework when inclement weather put paid to the opportunity of a sedate walk were a preview of the life Mary could expect if she were to remain unmarried. The pattern of her days was otherwise infrequently punctuated with the occasional pleasure of a card party or locally held dance or assembly; until the summer of 1746 that is, when everything changed – enter Captain the Honourable William Henry Cranstoun, the man who was 'to work the tragic mischief of her life'.

Chapter 2

'That damned villain, Cranstoun!'

The gallant cut of an officer's uniform was not an uncommon sight in Henley; however, as the younger son of the fifth Lord Cranstoun, a Scottish baron, whose mother, Lady Jane Kerr, happened to be the eldest daughter of the Marquis of Lothian, Captain William Henry Cranstoun held definite appeal. He presented himself as perfect husband material, on paper at least. Baptised at Crailing in Roxburghshire, on 12 August 1714, Cranstoun was the fifth of seven sons born to Lord and Lady Cranstoun, who also had five daughters. Of his four older brothers, James, later sixth Lord Cranstoun, was the only boy to survive into adulthood. Another son named William, along with Archibald and Alexander all died in infancy. There were two younger brothers, Charles and George, who survived to maturity, as did four of Cranstoun's five sisters: Anne; Mary; Jean and Elizabeth. A daughter named Jane is recorded as having 'died young'.

A little less than six years Mary's senior, and hailing from noble blood, it would seem from a contemporary account that Cranstoun's physical appearance was less than appealing:

'In his person he is remarkably ordinary, his stature is low, his face freckled and pitted with the smallpox, his eyes small and weak, his eyebrows sandy, and his shape no ways genteel; his legs are clumsy, and he has nothing in the least elegant in his manner.'

Yet something about Cranstoun, in his early thirties at the time he first met Mary, must have appealed to her; she may even have felt an affinity with someone who had been similarly ravaged by smallpox, and in spite of his literal shortcomings, his low stature, not to mention his clumsy legs, Mary was obviously receptive to the advances of this 'undersized spindleshanks'. And from the parental perspective, Mr and Mrs Blandy were more than happy to overlook the captain's financial shortcomings. The barony of Cranstoun was one that was somewhat on its uppers. With little more than his army pay to support himself and some sizeable debts to his name, run up in the pursuit of 'his many vicious and extravagant habits', Cranstoun was of threadbare worth. But the distinction of his Scottish title, which courtesy permitted him to assume, was certainly to prove an asset. As the son of a Scottish peer, the prospect of such a match blinded the Blandys, and the chance to marry their daughter to a man who could claim kinship with half the aristocracy of Scotland was an opportunity not to be passed up. As the old proverb has it, 'There are none so blind as those who will not see'.

Cranstoun was also locally well connected. He was the grand-nephew of General Lord Mark Kerr, who had bought Cranstoun's commission in the army. The purchase system, introduced in Queen Anne's reign, allowed rich, and often incompetent, officers to rise in the service to the rank of lieutenant colonel. His lordship was also an acquaintance of Francis Blandy, who, in his professional capacity may have been involved in the purchase of the house which Kerr had taken in Henley called The Paradise. The Blandys were certainly regular guests at the lordly table, and it was in the gardens of Paradise that Mary first met the man who would be instrumental in her downfall. Whether or not there were any apple trees flourishing in those gardens, there was certainly a serpent present in this particular Eden.

According to Mary's *Own Account*, her acquaintance with Cranstoun commenced in 1746, 'at Lord Mark Kerr's, in one of the summer months'. On this particular visit to Henley, Cranstoun was engaged on a recruiting drive, the gaps in the Hanoverian ranks needing to be filled after the final suppression of the Jacobite uprising, known as the '45 Rebellion, fought on Culloden Field. There is more than a suggestion that it was Mary's sizeable dowry which had first piqued Cranstoun's interest in her, he later admitting, supposedly in confidence to friends, that:

> 'On my coming to Henley, my first Enquiry was, what Ladies were the Toasts among the Men of Pleasure & Gaiety. Miss Blandy was named as the chief of them, and famed for a great Fortune.'

However, as at that time Mary was still engaged to 'Captain D.' who had won her affections in Bath, not to mention her father's necessary approval, Cranstoun was unable to make a play. But when he returned to Henley again the following summer of 1747 to stay with his esteemed grand-uncle, he learned that the affair had fallen through and that Mary, and her dowry, were once again available.

While the old Paradise house was demolished in the 1960s, in turn to be replaced by a housing estate in the 1970s, the Grade II listed boundary wall which surrounded the property still stands, and it was beyond this wall, at a summer garden party held by Lord Kerr, that Cranstoun first began his overtures to win the hand, and the fortune, of Miss Blandy. Indeed, Cranstoun was a man who did not need a second chance at making a first impression – especially when the stakes were so high. Whether or not he knew beforehand that Mary's parents, accompanied by their available daughter, would be amongst the guests invited that day, Cranstoun must have congratulated himself on the opportunity of a second bid for easy fortune, which, after the marriage vows had been uttered, he would be legally entitled to spend as he saw fit.

Doubtless, a speedy declaration of passion was made, and the proposal accepted with equal alacrity (perhaps Mary had a weakness for a man in uniform; she would not be the first!) as the following day Cranstoun made a formal request to Mary's father for his daughter's hand in marriage. Their snobbery brimming over at the expectation of an alliance with an ennobled family, Cranstoun's prospective in-laws were delighted. Though Cranstoun was obliged to absent himself from his intended, spending six weeks in Bath with his grand-uncle, on his return to Henley he was unreservedly welcomed into the Blandy family home, where he was to remain from late autumn for the next six months. Taking full advantage of the Blandy's hospitality, for 'no one was fonder of free quarters' Cranstoun was a charmer whose intentions, in spite of his title, were certainly less than honourable. The objective uppermost in his mind was the acquisition of Mary's dowry, and it was imperative that the course of true love ran smoothly; yet in spite of Cranstoun's ploy, it would seem that Mary's matrimonial expectations were to be thwarted once again.

The abundance of gossip and rumour which circulated around Henley assured that news of Mary's engagement to Cranstoun was soon common knowledge, furthered by her father, swollen with self-importance, making frequent pompous reference to 'my Lord of Crailing', while Mary's mother turned the subject of conversation to 'my Lady Cranstoun, my daughter's new mamma' with whomever she spoke. So, it was inevitable that Lord Kerr would eventually become aware of his grand-nephew's intentions. It was also inevitable that, as a man of honour, Kerr felt obliged to reveal to the Blandy's that their intended son-in-law, who had been basking in the adulation of both parents and daughter, was in fact already married, with a wife and child alive and well and living in Scotland.

The crushing disappointment of a second broken engagement with an officer of His Majesty's army must have been devastating for Mary, yet the bombshell came as no apparent surprise to her. Again, according to Mary's *Own Account*, when Cranstoun proposed, he had already intimated to her that he was involved in a lawsuit with a Scottish woman who claimed, with no legitimacy according to Cranstoun, that she was his wife. As Cranstoun was taking steps to have the marriage annulled, claiming that as it had been a private ceremony it had no validity in the eyes of the law, on these grounds the guileless Mary had provisionally accepted Cranstoun's proposal 'till the invalidity of the pretended marriage appeared to the whole world'. Needless to say, where the truth of the matter was concerned, the circumstances were otherwise, but that Cranstoun would happily have committed bigamy seemed certain, never mind the matter of abandoning his lawful wife and casting the stigma of bastardy upon his child. Clearly, Cranstoun was not a man to let the legally binding state of matrimony stand in the way of securing a fortune for himself, as would later become apparent; this was not the first time that the faithless captain had tried the same deception. It was said that before his arrival in Henley, Cranstoun had very nearly succeeded in capturing the hand of the daughter of a wealthy Leicestershire squire, but on learning of his past history, the timely intervention of that lady's father was to see Cranstoun unceremoniously sent packing. Undaunted, Cranstoun's later pursuit of Mary certainly proved he was a determined 'player' of the first degree. To anyone with eyes to see it, he had project written all over him.

Concerning his disputed marital status, on 22 May 1744 Cranstoun had been married, albeit in a private ceremony, to Anne Murray, the daughter of a Leith merchant who himself was the son of a baronet. The only witness present at the wedding was a single woman, and the clergyman, who had been bought by Cranstoun beforehand, and was not known to either Miss Murray or the witness. The covert nuptials concluded, the couple lived together 'in a private manner' until sometime in July, when Mrs Cranstoun went to stay at her uncle's house, Cranstoun staying with his own family until November, after which time he returned to London to resume his regimental duties. While they were apart husband and wife corresponded regularly, and Cranstoun also wrote letters to his own family and to the Murrays acknowledging that Anne had been his wife since May. He also wrote to his family that he was soon to be a father, as before the couple had parted, Anne had told Cranstoun that she was expecting his child. Though Lady Cranstoun had invited her daughter-in-law to Nether Crailing, the family seat in Roxburghshire, to await her confinement, Anne, who was a Catholic declined, fearing that the strong Presbyterian persuasions of her husband's family might be brought to bear upon her during her stay. So it was in Edinburgh, on 19 February 1745 that Cranstoun's daughter was born. In spite of her faith, Anne did agree to the baby being baptised by a minister of the established church. In the presence of several relations from both sides of the family, in Cranstoun's absence, one of his brothers held up the child for baptism, named for their mother, on Cranstoun's express instruction.

Even though members of both families had participated in the baptism of his daughter in the presence of his lawfully wedded wife, Cranstoun remained insistent that the marriage should be kept a closely guarded secret. His grounds were that if his marriage to Anne became public knowledge, in view of her religious and political affiliations (as well as her Catholicism, Anne's family had strong Jacobite connections), then his chances of preferment and promotion in the army would be seriously diminished. With this in mind, Cranstoun had further managed to persuade Anne that as his sole chance of promotion depended on the concealment of their marriage, as a safeguard against the truth coming out, it would be expedient if she were to write a letter, the wording of which was provided by Cranstoun, to the effect that she had never been his wife. Though she was reluctant, in the interest of furthering her husband's career, Anne agreed. But she was prudent enough to take some safeguarding measures of her own, perhaps intuitive to Cranstoun's potential, and soon to be discovered, perfidy. When her case seeking to uphold the validity of her marriage was later brought in court, though the letter of denial, in Anne's own handwriting, was produced, Cranstoun must have thought that such a written admission would be enough to sway the matter in his favour. However, Anne had kept his original draft, together with her faithless husband's letters of instruction; consequently, the credulity of his underhand ploy was thoroughly discredited, and Anne's status as Cranstoun's lawful wife was upheld. As will later become apparent, Mary Blandy would have done well to emulate Anne Cranstoun's caution with regards to incriminating correspondence, but here we jump ahead of her story.

With the fact of his 'secret marriage' disclosed, though Mary accepted Cranstoun's excuses masking the truth, the captain had his work cut out vindicating himself to Francis, which he managed by claiming that he and Anne had never actually married. Indeed, his explanation to the Blandys was the same as his defence presented to the Scottish Commissaries; that the lady was in fact his mistress. Although Cranstoun admitted to having made a promise of marriage to Anne, he maintained that his offer had rested on the condition that Anne would relinquish her faith and convert to Presbyterianism. According to his account, as Anne had refused to do so, and in double the timescale that Cranstoun had laid down, as she had reneged on her pledge, as far as he was concerned he was entirely freed from any obligation. Despite Cranstoun's defence, the birth of their daughter was nevertheless irrefutable proof that the couple had consummated the relationship, and entered into at least a form of 'irregular' marriage. In the eighteenth century such 'irregular' marriages were commonplace; if a man made a promise to marry a woman at a date in the future, and if the relationship was consummated before then, they were considered to be legally bound.

As one would expect, 'Mrs Cranstoun' vigorously defended her rights and her honour, and the legitimacy of her daughter. Presenting her case before the Commissioners at Edinburgh, which was the principal court in Scotland with exclusive jurisdiction in cases involving disputes over marriage, divorce and bastardy, Cranstoun may have placed his confidence in the sectarian prejudices of the Scottish law courts in view of Anne's Catholicism. Yet after examination of the copious letters exchanged between 'husband and wife' the court ruled in Anne's favour. On 1 March 1748, it was decreed that Cranstoun and Anne were legally married persons and that the child was their lawful and legitimate daughter. A crushing judgement for Cranstoun, and not least from a financial point of view as on 7 April, following, the court awarded Anne, as Cranstoun's lawful wife, an annuity of forty pounds for herself, and ten pounds for their daughter, in addition awarding a further forty pounds to Anne in costs, with Cranstoun ordered to pay nearly sixty pounds in court costs. Worse still, with more than half his army pay sequestered for the maintenance of his wife and child, shortly after the treaty negotiations for the peace of Aix-la-Chapelle were concluded, his regiment was disbanded and Cranstoun was reduced to half-pay. This was a typical money-saving scheme by governments then and since. His need for money was therefore great; yet if only he could secure Mary's hand, and her enormous dowry, all of his problems would be solved.

Despite the fact that Francis Blandy himself had not been entirely truthful with regards to the confirmed amount of Mary's dowry – in fact, the sum was closer to four thousand pounds rather than the ten thousand touted, though still a not inconsiderable amount – he had been understandably and justifiably incensed when he had learned that Cranstoun was not a bachelor. He must also have been irked by the fact that he had fallen for Cranstoun's con. However, Cranstoun was adamant that he would continue to contest the validity of his supposed marriage, and as 'the Court of first instance, as was not unprecedented, had erred' he had been advised that there was every chance that an appeal against the judgment to the Court of Sessions – there was a limited right of appeal to the Edinburgh Commissary Court – would prove successful. He also swore his eternal fidelity to Mary.

For her part, Mary's faith in her lover held strong, even after Anne Cranstoun, now aware of her husband's romantic attachment in Henley, wrote a warning letter to Mary, enclosing a copy of the Court's decree in her favour. It made no difference. Whether or not Mary was hopeful for Cranstoun's appeal, or simply determined not to let this opportunity of marriage slip through her fingers, and fall prey to the 'dreadful stigma of spinsterhood', her unfaltering loyalty was the mark of her future strength of feeling; an infatuation that would see her throw all caution and common sense to the wind.

Needless to say, winning back the confidence and approval of Francis Blandy was a different proposition entirely, but when the matter came to a head and Cranstoun was confronted, he was persuasive enough to dupe the old man into believing his assertions, swearing on his oath that 'As I have a soul to be saved,' that 'I am not, nor ever was [a married man]'. Maintaining that the supposed Mrs Cranstoun had wilfully misrepresented her case to the Scottish Courts, concerning his grand-uncle's timely intervention, this was explained away as malicious interference, the upshot of an old quarrel between them, long since forgotten by Cranstoun and 'buried in oblivion', but for which his lordship still unaccountably held a grudge. At this point, one has to question Francis's incredulity in accepting this as an explanation. If Lord Kerr really did still harbour any old enmity toward his grand-nephew, on whatever grounds, would he have been inclined to repeatedly invite his errant relation as a guest to his house, or ask that he accompany him on a six week trip to Bath? Perhaps in the same way that Mary was blinkered to Cranstoun's real intentions and obvious lies, likewise her father may have been all too ready to swallow the disguised deceits and excuses, Francis Blandy after all 'in the vanity of his heart ha[d] been heard to say he hoped still to live to be a grandfather to a lord'. And his anger may have been further ameliorated by the esteem in which his wife held Cranstoun, the captain from the very first successful in charming Mary's mother with his winning ways; as Cranstoun was to state himself, 'nor was the Mother less fond of me than the Daughter'. Though Anne Blandy had been initially devastated by the revelation of Cranstoun's married state, believing that 'her poor Polly was ruined', she nevertheless proved herself eager to clutch at any explanation, however specious, her sympathies for Cranstoun such that she was persuasive enough to turn her husband to the same bent. We can imagine Francis Blandy being subject to some imploring scenes acted out at the Hart Street mansion, pleas on Cranstoun's behalf, on the part of both mother and daughter.

At length, on the acceptance of his word, Cranstoun was allowed to remain as a guest in the Blandy household, until such time as the outcome of the further legal proceedings he had instigated north of the border were known. It was nevertheless made clear that Cranstoun's presence at The Paradise would be objectionable, and in view of Lord Kerr's anger at the apparent indifference with which his well-meaning revelation had been met, presumably the Blandys were no longer welcome guests either. The upshot of this, as well as being to the Blandy's social detriment, was the loss of the opportunity to learn of any further direct details of their prospective son-in-law's misdeeds from a reliable source; a decided disadvantage, but one which Cranstoun could turn to his favour.

Cranstoun continued to freeload off the Blandy's hospitality until the spring of 1748, after which he went to London, presumably once again to resume his regimental duties on the outbreak of the War of the Austrian Succession. During this absence, Mary's father consented to the continuation of the engagement, until such time as the legal position of Cranstoun's 'marriage' was resolved; in the meantime, the couple kept up a frequent correspondence. However, Cranstoun's spare time may not have been solely devoted in writing letters to his fiancée. He was spending time in the company of 'a lady then enjoying his protection in town', who may or may not have been the same 'Miss Capel' who, as would later be revealed, had previously borne Cranstoun a child. Needless to say, Mary was entirely ignorant of this liaison.

After Cranstoun's removal from the Blandys' domestic sphere, Mary's life of provincial gentility continued much the same as ever, and some time after her fiancé's departure, mother and daughter paid a visit to a friend, a Mrs Pocock who resided at Turville Court, a country estate a little over eight miles from Henley. Their pleasant sojourn was interrupted however when Anne Blandy was taken ill, and it was initially feared that her condition might prove life threatening. Drawing again from Mary's *Own Account*, in her supposedly near-death state, Anne Blandy's constant plea was 'let Cranstoun be sent for'. Ever the opportunist, Cranstoun obliged, and hastening from his re-posting in Southampton, once he had arrived at Turville Court, Mary's mother soon rallied, declaring that now Cranstoun had come, she would soon be well again; 'This I owe to you, my dear Cranstoun; your coming has given me new health and fresh spirits'. Her insistence that she would take no medicine other than that administered by Cranstoun's own hand would prove prophetic however.

In view of his wife's condition, Francis Blandy had also been hastily summoned to Turville Court, though when he arrived he was nettled on learning of the 'great expense' that her care had incurred, and insisted on Anne's immediate return to Henley where 'neither the physician's fees nor the apothecary's journeys could be so expensive'; a penny-pinching decision to which he held firm, regardless of whether or not his wife was even well enough to travel. With pecuniary concerns clearly uppermost in his mind, the entire party, including Cranstoun, returned to the house at Hart Street, and on the strength of Anne Blandy's continued ill health, Cranstoun managed to inveigle another six month stay at the family home, of course at no cost to himself, leeching bed and board until he was ready to return to London, his regiment by this time having broken camp at Southampton.

While Anne Blandy would remain, albeit deludedly, Cranstoun's champion, before his departure there were obvious frictions in the household. Mary was to make a telling reference to her father's attitude during Cranstoun's further extended stay, that he was sometimes 'very rude' to his 'guest'; was Francis Blandy simply aggravated by the further expense of providing for Cranstoun's accommodation, again, or did he harbour some suspicion of the captain's real intentions? As Cranstoun saw it, Francis Blandy's growing resentment, even mistrust, was not an insurmountable obstacle, certainly if he could be removed from the equation altogether. And in the lovelorn Mary Blandy, he had found a compliant scapegoat whom he could manipulate into performing long-distance patricide, without even dirtying his own hands; hands which he must have greedily rubbed together.

Chapter 3

A Fleet Wedding?

I n the spring of 1749, a few months after Cranstoun's most recent departure from Hart Street, with the roads no longer rendered seas of mud by the winter weather, Mary accompanied her mother to London. The trip was undertaken with a view to seeking medical advice as Anne Blandy's health was still a cause for concern. While in town, mother and daughter stayed with Anne Blandy's brother, Henry Stevens, Serjeant at Law to the Doctors' Commons, a society of lawyers practising civil law in London. Naturally, as Cranstoun was still in town himself, this afforded him the opportunity of visiting mother and daughter, and further ingratiating himself with Mrs Blandy – were that ever necessary. Wasting no time, Cranstoun turned up on the morning of their arrival and paid court every day thereafter. On one such visit, Mary's *Own Account* mentions that Cranstoun was accompanied by his elder brother, James, now sixth Lord Cranstoun, he having succeeded to the title on the death of his father in 1727. While Mary failed to make any mention of the Lord James's feelings concerning the matter of his younger brother's ongoing matrimonial debacle in the Scottish courts, we can assume that Anne Blandy would have been delighted beyond measure to receive such an exalted caller, and one with whom she presumed she would soon be familially connected by her daughter's marriage.

Anne Blandy's brother clearly felt otherwise. Falling far short of being beguiled by Cranstoun's noble connections, aware of the ongoing legal situation, Henry Stevens refused to invite Mary's fiancé to dinner, and in spite of his sister's tears, remained steadfast in his disapproval. Weeping and apologetic, Anne Blandy took 'dear Mr. Cranstoun' by the hand, declaring, 'I am sorry you should be so affronted by any of my family, but I dare not ask you to stay to dinner. However, come to me as often as you can in my own apartment; in a morning I am always alone.' Keen to avoid any domestic discord, mother and daughter were obliged to entertain the captain within the confines of Anne Blandy's rooms, but there was still the risk of affronting their host. Fortunate, then, that Anne Blandy's good friend, Mrs Pocock of Turville Court, also kept a townhouse in St James's Square, where she was more than happy to receive Cranstoun. No surprise then, according to

Mary, that 'Hither Mr. Cranstoun perpetually came, when he understood that I was there'.

It is clear that during their stay neither Mary, her mother or Cranstoun for that matter were aware that Francis Blandy himself had travelled to London on business. But fickle fate, as is so often the way, contrived for their paths to cross. After pleasantly dining one day with Mrs Pocock, the party decided to order a coach for an afternoon outing, but who should they run into while driving down the Strand than Francis Blandy himself. The following encounter was acrimonious to say the least; 'For God's sake, Mrs. Pocock, what do you with this rubbish?' exclaimed Mary's father. 'Rubbish!' Mrs Pocock remonstrated, 'Your wife, your daughter, and one who may be your son?' 'Ay,' replied Francis Blandy, caustically adding, 'They are very well matched; 'tis a pity they should ever be asunder!' At this point, Cranstoun interjected, 'God grant they never may,' adding the barb 'don't you say amen, papa?' 'Papa' must have felt that Cranstoun was twisting the knife; seething, he declined Mrs Pocock's invitation to join them, and as soon as his business permitted, Francis Blandy left London and returned post-haste to Henley.

Cranstoun was indeed foolish to bait Francis Blandy with such words, but he may have spoken in the heat of the moment, or perhaps he was already confident enough in the plan he had now formed in his mind. Feeling the obvious animosity that was growing toward him from that quarter, there was the decided risk that Mary's father would force the couple to break off the match at any time. Cranstoun could not afford, literally, to let Mary's fortune slip through his fingers. Aware that the clock was ticking, rather than waiting for his legal wrangle to be resolved in the Scottish courts, of which there was no favourable guarantee, circumventing the need for parental approval, and presenting Francis Blandy with a *fait accompli*, Cranstoun proposed to Mary the solution of a 'secret marriage'. After all, as far as Cranstoun was concerned he was free to go through with another such ceremony.

In this respect, a 'Fleet marriage' would have been one option. Though famed as a debtors' prison, by a curious legislative quirk, the 'Liberty of the Fleet' – that is the prison and the surrounding area – was exempt from the necessity of reading marriage banns – the public announcement of an impending marriage – as dictated by the Marriage Duty Act passed in 1696. Conventionally a couple, where both parties were free to marry, would have to wait several weeks while the banns 'went up', but within the Liberty of the Fleet a marriage could be legally celebrated with haste, and outside the precincts of a church – indeed many such marriage services were conducted in the inns and taverns falling within the Liberty. Another advantage was that the costs of a church wedding were also avoided. 'Tack'd together' by one of the Couple-Beggars, the term applied to ministers (of varying denominations) who had been defrocked and subsequently made a living from offering a range of services, including marriages, at a reduced fee and undercutting what would have been demanded by a legitimate minister. Though these 'irregular' marriages performed by Fleet Clergy were accepted as valid, not all marriages were necessarily above board; recorded cases of bigamy in the Fleet show that some 'bachelors' and 'spinsters' wed several times before being caught, and it was not unknown for Couple-Beggars to provide, for a fee of course, marriage certificates for women to use as evidence of respectability, no questions asked. The notorious practice of clandestine Fleet Marriages was finally put paid to with the passing of The Marriage Act 1753, full title 'An Act for the Better Preventing of Clandestine Marriage'; popularly known as Lord Hardwicke's Marriage Act, the legislation coming into force on 25 March 1754.

Though Mary appeared susceptibly pliant in yielding to Cranstoun's suggestions, whether or not she unwittingly played out his later murderous intentions, in this instance however her head did rule her heart. Refusing point blank to countenance the idea of a marriage without her father's consent, whether it be 'according to the usage of the Church of England' or not, showing no want of propriety Mary insisted that Cranstoun first undertake to obtain legal opinion from the Solicitor-General for Scotland questioning the validity of such a union, in view of the circumstances of his on-going appeal, before she would take a single step toward the altar (or the public bar!) Whether or not Cranstoun ever made any such application to the Solicitor-General, or simply strung Mary along to think that he had done so, no response from north of the border was forthcoming. Yet Cranstoun, revealing his true murky colours, was later to state in his own account of the affair that the couple were in fact married, and at Mary's request! Cranstoun was to cite Mary's reasoning for the proposal as one of necessity, 'lest he [Cranstoun] should prove ungrateful to her after so material an intimacy'. The inference here would suggest that Mary and Cranstoun had already consummated their relationship, though this is a matter of conjecture; would Mary have been foolish enough to risk pregnancy out of wedlock?

There were contraceptive choices available in the eighteenth century, though they were often costly and there was no guarantee of reliability. But this did nothing to diminish the thriving customer base enjoyed by 'Mrs Phillips' who was the proprietress of the Green Canister, in Half Moon

Street (now Bedford Street) in Covent Garden. Astutely located, at the time Covent Garden – or 'the great square of Venus' – was the prime location for Georgian London's sex trade, and during her time as a courtesan, Phillips had clearly learned, as well as 'turned' a trick or two. Handbills printed to advertise her wares were given out to prospective customers in the street by link boys, keen to earn a few extra pennies, and amongst the most popular items touted were 'preservatives', or, more widely speaking, condoms. Made from a sheep's intestine, the standard length on offer was between seven and eight inches, secured with a coloured ribbon around the base. In addition to condoms, which at the time were reusable, the Green Canister would also have carried variations of the contraceptive sponge, a piece of natural sponge or linen with a length of ribbon stitched to it. Soaked in a dilute solution of lemon juice, or more commonly vinegar, this was a vague barrier method incorporating a natural spermicide and favoured by prostitutes, but also employed by 'ordinary' women, especially those desirous of a break from childbearing. Not so different from a modern sex shop, the Green Canister also stocked a comprehensive range of 'devices' catering to every sexual whim, though obviously in the eighteenth century, batteries were not included!

Whilst the extent of Mary and Cranstoun's enjoyment of one another's company is open to question, for her part, Anne Blandy was certainly enjoying her stay in London. Along with the opportunity to entertain at Mrs Pocock's townhouse, busy days were filled with all the pleasures and spectacles that the capital could afford in the spring of 1749. The 'Old' Westminster Bridge was nearing completion, surviving two earth tremors that year, the precursors to several seismic events in 1750, the so-called 'Year of Earthquakes', the first of which on the morning of 8 March 'rattled and clattr'd' windowpanes 'as upon the Explosion of a Cannon'. Another 'explosive' event was the first official performance of Handel's *Music for the Royal Fireworks*. Held in Green Park on 27 April, the Orchestral Suite in five movements was composed to accompany the royal celebrations in commemoration of the Peace of Aix-la-Chapelle which had ended the War of the Austrian Succession, the treaty responsible for the drastic cut in Cranstoun's army salary. The build-up for this unprecedented event was huge; top-notch concerts open to the general public were virtually unheard of at the time and the anticipation and excitement was so great that tickets were even sold-out for a public rehearsal held in the Vauxhall Pleasure Gardens. Around 12,000 people flocked to the official performance held in Green Park, resulting in a traffic jam that closed London Bridge for several hours.

Unfortunately, the entertainment finished early when disaster struck and the staging and pavilion caught fire, the architect of the pavilion, Giovanni Niccolo Servandoni so incensed by the mismanagement of the pyrotechnics that he drew his sword on one of the organisers.

In whatever manner Anne Blandy spent her time, and indeed her money while in the capital, according to Mary her mother revealed to her toward the end of their stay that she was in debt to the tune of £40. To give an idea of the sum in relative worth, this would amount to nearly £6,000 in today's money. As demonstrated by her husband's carping and penny-pinching over the medical expenses when she was believed to be dangerously ill, it comes as no surprise that Anne Blandy was more than a little reluctant to divulge the extent of the amount she owed, and in Mary's words, that 'she durst not inform my father of it'. But her darling Cranstoun was to come to the rescue. Loaning Mrs Blandy the required amount, though where the indigent Captain managed to magic such a sum of money from remains a mystery. The magnanimous Cranstoun delivered the cash directly into Anne Blandy's own hands. Rendered speechless with relief and gratitude, 'she squeezed his hand and burst into tears'. Cranstoun then kissed her, and said, 'Remember, 'tis a son, and therefore don't make yourself uneasy; you can't lie under any obligation to me'.

Though the impetus behind the trip to London had been to seek a medical opinion, while it would seem that Anne Blandy had certainly experimented with some therapy of the retail variety, it would be wrong to assume that she had run up the entire sizeable debt as a consequence of a shopping addiction alone. Mary's *Own Account* tells of a different, less indulgent cause, namely that the lion's share of the debt was owing to the monies laid out to fund the hospitalities and entertainments Cranstoun himself had made free with while staying at the family home in Henley. Prior to their departure from town, Anne exonerated all of her London debts, which amounted to £10, and though this was still a sizeable sum, the remaining £30 she was obliged to pay on her return to Hart Street, 'to the footman, for fowls, butter, eggs, wine, and other provisions, brought into the house', the provision of which was 'chiefly on account of entertainments, by him [Cranstoun]'. Clearly, when it came to spending someone else's money, Cranstoun's tastes were extravagant.

In view of Henry Stevens strictures with regards to Cranstoun and his attachment to his niece, when the time came to return home, to save embarrassment and difficulty all round it was thought best that Mary and her mother depart from Anne's sister's house in Watling Street, and it was from there that they both took their leave of Cranstoun, parting 'in a very moving manner' before setting out for Henley the following day. Having arrived in 'due time' Mary wrote to Cranstoun, as he had requested, giving him an account of their safe arrival, and thanking him 'in the strongest terms, for his late extraordinary favour'. Mary must have assumed that Cranstoun understood that her gratitude in respect of her mother's pecuniary 'bailout' also extended to the additional 'favour' of the five guineas Cranstoun had given to Mary herself, intended as a provision for travel expenses 'in case the council should think a private marriage proper'. In other words, if a favourable response were forthcoming from Scotland, Mary would have sufficient money 'to come up in a post-chaise to London and meet him [Cranstoun] there, with all possible expedition'. Clearly, this refutes Cranstoun's later assertion that a 'secret marriage', at Mary's behest, had already taken place.

Some six months after Mary and her mother had returned home, perhaps exacerbated by Cranstoun's absence, or a lack of decent shops in Henley, Anne Blandy became seriously ill. In the early hours of 28 September, she 'complained of a pain in her bowel', and though she 'lay pretty easy till six', a messenger was dispatched to fetch Mr Norton, the Henley apothecary, who habitually attended to the Blandy family's medical needs. Having bled his patient, the debilitating eighteenth century go-to treatment for any variety of ailments, Norton further prescribed some 'gentle physic', and while his patient seemed to improve a little, when her brother John, the Reverend Stevens, arrived – he happened to be in the town at the time, enjoying a game of bowls at the Bell Inn – he found his sister 'greatly indisposed'. It was hoped that, as before when she was taken ill on her stay with Mrs Pocock at Turville Court, though the complaint was of a different nature, Mary's mother would nevertheless recover. Unfortunately, this was not to be the case. Francis Blandy, for once not heeding the cost, acquiesced in summoning the eminent Dr Addington from Reading to consult on his ailing wife. Suffice it to say that we will hear more of Addington in a later chapter, his part in Mary's story pivotal to his future as well as hers.

After the doctor's arrival at Hart Street, despite, or perhaps because of his ministrations – in line with common practice the patient was once again bled – it was obvious that Anne was sinking fast. Even the administration of further 'physic' had no effect. This was understandable, if one of the popular tonics of the day were prescribed, either brandy, mint water or 'Sir Walter Raleigh's Cordial', a herbal concoction with the comparable alcoholic strength of absinthe. Seeing that the end was near, Henry Stevens, Anne's other brother who had proved such a disapproving host in London, was summoned from his country house at nearby Culham Court. With her family gathered at the bedside, to the very end, Anne maintained her faith in the Lord, and in Cranstoun, her last words to her husband, that 'Mary has set her heart upon Cranstoun; when I am gone, let no one set you against the match'. One would have thought that as a comfort to his dying wife, Francis would at least have given the appearance of acquiescing to this final request, yet his response was that the matter would only be decided once the 'unhappy affair in Scotland' was concluded, and Cranstoun's ambiguous marital status resolved.

Around nine o'clock on the evening of 30 September, Anne breathed her last. She was 49 years old. Laid to rest in the chancel of the church where she had been married, and where her darling 'Polly' had been baptised, who amongst the mourners then present could have foreseen the circumstances in which, less than two years later, they would be gathered again for the interment of Francis's body alongside that of his wife?

Judging by the contemporary accounts, it would seem that Anne had died as a result of complications arising from intestinal inflammation. An unfortunate cause of death, not least for the deceased herself, but because of the implications and allegations later levelled against Mary in the light of her father's own demise. Obviously, her symptoms were not indicative of a repeat of the disorder which she had suffered while staying at Turville Court, namely 'a complaint in her breast' for which she had sought medical advice in London. It may have been that she was suffering from a chronic condition, stemming from some earlier obstetric problem, as Mary was later to recount that:

'when my mother was in labour of me, she received a hurt; which made me apprehensive of ill consequences, which either the cholick [sic], which was her present disorder, or any obstructions in the parts contiguous to those which are the seat of that distemper, happened.'

Of course, in 1749 there were no wholly effective means for determining a definite diagnosis of an internal complaint, or treatment for that matter. Surgery was a last resort, and even the most exalted of patients who endured operative procedures – without anaesthesia – were subject to the same risks as anyone else. Caroline of Ansbach, George II's queen, was one such case in point. In 1737, she underwent the trauma of surgery for a strangulated umbilical hernia, the legacy of her ninth and final pregnancy. In the gruesome operation, the doctors sliced away the decayed flesh, in the process completely opening her bowels and causing catastrophic damage. Incredibly, in spite of the agonies she was suffering, Caroline's sense of humour did not desert her; when the wig of one of the surgeons bending over her abdomen was set alight by a candle flame, the queen was sent into such paroxysms of laughter that she begged him to stay his scalpel until she had recovered her composure.

Whatever the cause of Anne's death, it was apparent that she died of natural causes; Mary knew full well that in her mother Cranstoun had the staunchest of supporters. She would, therefore, have been foolish indeed to have poisoned her (and for what reason?) as her later detractors were to suggest.

With the household plunged into mourning, as condolences were received, an old friend of Anne's and neighbour of the family, a Mrs Mounteney, came to visit and commiserate with the bereaved. Mrs Mounteney was also Mary's godmother, and on her deathbed, Anne had magnanimously suggested that if her husband should ever 'discover an inclination to marry her' that he had her blessing. Yet Mrs Mounteney was to play an entirely different role to that of prospective step-mother to Mary, as her appearance in the witness box would later testify.

Naturally, Mary wrote to Cranstoun, still in London, of the sad news of her mother's passing, and implored him to return to Henley. Cranstoun replied that while his most fervent wish was to be by her side at such a time, he could not, however, undertake to make the journey as he was confined to his lodgings for fear of the bailiffs. Whether or not it was the truth or a means of exacting ready cash, in the circumstances Cranstoun suggested that Mary borrow the necessary money to relieve him of the current sticky financial situation in which he found himself. This Mary promptly did, but borrowed the necessary amount from Mrs Mounteney, her godmother, rather than requesting the sum from her father. Forwarding £15 on to Cranstoun, once freed of his immediate debt, he travelled to Henley, where he was to remain for some weeks.

Francis Blandy must have been greatly affected by the death of his wife, for his grief was such that, initially, he raised no objection to the captain's resumed residence, in spite of his previous animosity toward Cranstoun, and the inevitable costs that his further stay would likely occasion. But in time the old man's patience wore as thin as Cranstoun's finances. Soon Mary was complaining about the 'unkind things' which her father said to both herself and her fiancé, and the atmosphere at Hart Street must have been uncomfortable to say the least. With no movement or news with regard to Cranstoun's marital litigation, the only word forthcoming from Scotland was the 'very civil' letter of condolence penned by Cranstoun's mother, along with the gift of a kippered salmon, which according to Lady Cranstoun was known to be most beneficial to those grieving the loss of a loved one. There is no mention as to whether this strange recommendation eased Francis Blandy's sorrow, but for sure he was fast losing faith in Cranstoun. As long as Mary's mother was alive, she had remained his firmest adherent, but with her passing, as she was no longer available to fight Cranstoun's corner, the obvious doubts and suspicions which Francis harboured, once held in check by his wife's mollifying influence, began to grow. Making no secret of his feelings, Francis Blandy acted on them. Barring Cranstoun from Hart Street, he was forbidden to enter the house, it would be nearly a year before he and Mary were to meet again.

Chapter 4

No Performance No Pay

Though the lovers were now parted, before his banishment from the Blandy household, Cranstoun had astutely taken the opportunity of planting the seed of the idea which would ultimately burgeon into Mary's manipulated murder of her father.

It was clear that even the most persuasive entreaties would not alter Francis Blandy's attitude, be they the implorings of his daughter or the dissembling efforts of Cranstoun himself. Another course of action was required. Before he left Henley, Cranstoun and Mary had one last assignation in the grounds of Park Place, a country house surrounded by lovely gardens just across the Thames in Remenham. Long afterwards, this favourite trysting spot of theirs (the engagement was after all now in its third year), where the couple often met, later became romantically known as 'Miss Blandy's Walk'. It was in the grounds of this opulent Palladian mansion that Cranstoun first broached his diabolical plan, and we can imagine Mary having hung on her lover's every word when he first 'acquainted her of the great skill of the famous Mrs Morgan,' a cunning woman who was known to him in Scotland, and who could solve all their problems.

Mrs Morgan had apparently supplied Cranstoun in the past with a certain powder, 'which she called love-powders', and which Cranstoun had once taken himself. The term 'love' as applied to the powders in this instance refers to 'affection' rather than any amorous influence, though there were powders available which, it was believed, could be employed to induce such an outcome if so desired; Horace Bleackley, in his *Some Distinguished Victims of the Scaffold*, published in 1905, in connection to Mary's case included a contemporary advertisement for a 'Love Philtre' which ran as follows:

'THE FAMOUS LOVE-POWDER, OR LOVE-DROPS.

'Sold for Five Shillings a bottle, at the Golden-Ball, in Stone-Cutters-Street, Fleet-Market.

'Any person that is in love with a man, and he won't return it, let her come to me, and I'll make him glad of her, and thank ye to boot, by only giving him a little of these love drops, it will make him that he can't rest without her. And the like, if a man is in love with a young woman, and she won't comply, let him give her a little of this liquor of love, and she will not be able to rest without him. If a woman has got a husband that goes astray, let her give him a few of these drops, and it will make him, rest at home, and never desire to go no more. And the like with a man if his wife goes astray, it will make her that she will never desire no other man.

'This liquor is the study of a Jesuit, one Mr. Delore, and is sold by his nephew, Mr. John Delore, and I promise very fair, if it don't perform all I say, I'll have nothing for my pains; and if any young master has debauched a servant, and after won't have her, let her give him a little of this liquor, and if he don't marry her, I'll have nothing for it; therefore, I promise very fair, no performance no pay.'

Whether or not Mrs Morgan promised 'no performance no pay' apparently the proven positive effects of the powders she had previously supplied to Cranstoun were felt immediately by the captain. Miraculously compelled to forgive a former friend with whom he had quarrelled and had intended never to speak to again, how could the powers of the powders possibly be in doubt? While Cranstoun's claim as to the effectiveness of these 'love powders' must be dismissed as phooey, not least because his fabrication was intended to lull Mary into the belief that they were efficacious as well as harmless, the credence placed in such supernatural concoctions might seem ridiculous now, but it was not always so. Cranstoun's supposed Scottish supplier was one of many who could tentatively be placed into the category of folk healer, in England and Scotland also known as 'cunning folk'. Selling spells and charms was the mainstay of their profession, stemming from the Medieval period, or even earlier, and carried through to the early twentieth century. Legions of ordinary people relied on the services of these cunning folk, often in lieu of the expensive and often unreliable treatments offered by doctors. Spells and charms were made to order, and employed to resolve a myriad undesirable situations: to combat malevolent witchcraft; to locate criminals, missing persons or stolen property; to tell fortunes as well as to seek out hidden treasure; and of course to influence matters of the heart. And if the contraceptives mentioned in the previous chapter had proved ineffective, a cunning person could also be called upon to whip up a herbal abortifacient, the centuries-old concoctions of Pennyroyal and Tansy held to be reliable. At the time, procuring or performing an abortion was against the law, not to mention the risk to life if the dose was incorrectly prepared or administered, a defence cited in the face of many poisoning indictments brought against 'reluctant fathers' in cases where 'apparent' abortion attempts resulted in the death of both the mother and unborn child.

Typically, the benefits that cunning folk offered to their local community were facilitated by what they claimed to be their own 'magical powers', and it may have been the whiff of witchcraft attached to their practices that brought Mary up short with regards to her protestations that she had no faith in such things – she had, after all, been instructed by her mother 'in the principles of religion and piety, according to the rites and ceremonies of the Church of England'. Even so, though this was the 'Age of Reason', attitudes were nevertheless credulous. John Wesley believed in poltergeists and Dr Johnson investigated the Cock Lane ghost. Whether or not Cranstoun emphatically believed in Mrs Morgan's supposed 'magical' prowess, he was insistent in the promised effects of such a philtre, and confidently asserted that 'If I had any of these powders,' he would without hesitation 'put them into something Mr. Blandy should drink'. However, for the time being, there the matter rested.

Cranstoun bided his time in London, but eventually, put pen to paper. Possibly he had suggested that Mary play on her mother's deathbed request in an attempt to soften up her father, or perhaps Mary's own continued implorings had worn the old man down, for when Cranstoun wrote to Francis Blandy on 1 August 1750, asking that he be allowed to visit, Mary's father relented, though with little enthusiasm, agreeing 'He must come, I suppose'.

Cranstoun duly arrived in Henley, but regrettably without the hoped-for assurances that a satisfactory verdict in the matter of his Scottish marriage was close to being reached. Francis Blandy was ill-disposed to conceal his contempt. Without the placatory presence of his wife, the visit proved unpleasant for all concerned, the domestic situation in the Hart Street house deteriorating from tense to strained to insupportable. Mealtimes were particularly difficult, as Mary 'seldom rose from the table without tears'. In this acrimonious atmosphere, whenever possible, Mary's father opted to spend his evenings at the local coffee-house, significantly limiting his contact with his unwelcome guest.

As the awkwardness and obvious avoidances continued, Cranstoun clearly thought that the time was right to implement the initial stage of his plan to 'remove' the parental obstacle to his gaining a fortune. Cranstoun began to pressure Mary. 'Why will you not permit me to give your father some of the powders which I formerly mentioned?' He offered the assurance that 'they are quite innocent, and will do him no harm if they did not produce the desired effect'. The conversation was cut short however when Francis entered the room, and the perennial uncomfortable silence resumed.

The following morning, Mary found her father in his study, as ever very much out of humour. Closing the door and leaving the old man to his mood, the tearful Mary went into the parlour to join Cranstoun for breakfast and began to make tea. As she went to fetch the sugar, Cranstoun said, 'I will now put in some of the powder – upon my soul it will not hurt him.' Clearly, Mary was still troubled by the suggestion of employing such measures and remonstrated, 'Don't do it, Cranstoun; it will make me uneasy, and can do you no good.' To which Cranstoun replied, 'It can do no hurt, and therefore I will mix it.' This Cranstoun did, but when Mary returned to the tea table, intent on throwing the tea away, at that moment her father entered the room. She could hardly tip away his drink without arousing suspicion, and before she could come up with a plausible excuse for doing so, he had taken his first sip. Though he continued throughout breakfast-time 'much out of humour', afterwards retiring again to his study, by dinner time, to the wonderment of his pensive daughter, incredibly he appeared in the best of moods, and even more unexpectedly 'continued so all the time Mr. Cranstoun stayed with him'. What had affected this turn of favour is impossible to know; as he suffered no immediate ill effects, the powders Cranstoun incorporated into the old man's tea could have been nothing more than a harmless substance, an innocuous substitute intended to demonstrate to Mary that if she were to administer the same in future, no harm would befall her father. However, if the powder were indeed of a more sinister nature, this may give us the answer, as arsenic does present itself as something of a 'medicinal double-edged sword'. In the past employed as both a therapeutic agent as well as a poison, at one time used as a tonic, arsenic was prescribed to treat a variety of systemic illnesses. Researchers have recently found that arsenic and its derivatives have shown some promise in treating a variety of cancers, and the development of new uses for medicinal arsenic are on-going in clinical trials today. Although arsenic has been known as a poison for thousands of years there have long been reports of beneficial effects, albeit limited to the outset of its administration, and it may have been that an initial dose proved beneficial to Francis, temporarily alleviating some of the symptoms of the various ailments from which he was known to suffer and that this circumstance accounted for his improved mood. Curative coincidences aside, Cranstoun must have congratulated himself on the decidedly favourable turn in Francis's frame of mind. How could Mary possibly doubt his suggested course of action now?

It does seem odd, however, that at this juncture Cranstoun would choose to impart a further 'secret' – above and beyond that of his Scottish wife – which could have seriously jeopardised his relationship with Mary. Perhaps fearing another untimely exposure, like that made by Lord Kerr to Mary's parents concerning his marriage, Cranstoun admitted to Mary that a year prior to their meeting, as a consequence of an assignation with a 'Miss Capel' whom he had met in London, that he was, in fact, father to another daughter. Cranstoun told Mary that his confession was made at the insistence of his conscionable friends, but it is equally likely that, with the whiff of the impending dowry he stood to gain, Cranstoun was being blackmailed. But with no ready means of paying off a would-be extortionist, he sought to circumvent any compromising revelation by making a clean breast of it and telling the truth himself (something of a novelty for Cranstoun). Mary was magnanimous in her understanding, the affair had after all (according to Cranstoun) taken place a year before they had first met, but nevertheless she admonished him, saying that, 'Your follies, Cranstoun, have been very great; but I hope you see them'. After he had fully acknowledged his 'penitence and shame', Mary made free with her forgiveness, but on the condition that Cranstoun never 'repeat these follies now after our acquaintance'. To all appearances, Cranstoun was chastened. Naming himself 'a villain' he made good on his apparent contrition and told Mary that 'you alone can make me happy in this world; and, by following your example, I hope I shall be happy in the next'. Hollow words indeed, as Mary was soon to discover, for Cranstoun had indeed proved himself a 'villain' *since* their engagement, as at that very time he was currently involved in an illicit affair with another woman.

A day or two after Cranstoun's admission, when he was out of the house, Mary engaged in some light domestic duties, perhaps in anticipation of her 'wifely' role. Entering Cranstoun's room 'to look out his linnen [sic]' for her maid to wash, the usual soiled clothing pile was missing from the table. Mary took it upon herself to check Cranstoun's trunk; an innocent enough supposition on the part of his wife-to-be, and as the key was in the lock she went ahead and opened it. However, rather than dirty laundry, the first thing that greeted Mary was an opened letter in an unfamiliar hand – Cranstoun was apparently in the habit of passing his correspondence, unopened, for

Mary to read, in a demonstration of their open and trusting relationship. This particular missive had obviously slipped the net. Of recent date, the letter addressed to Cranstoun had been received from a lady who had apparently been 'enjoying his protection in town'. The inference here need not be questioned further and was certainly clear to Mary.

Replacing the letter and locking the trunk, Mary put the key in her pocket and went back downstairs to her father's study and asked him to come into breakfast. 'No, not till Cranstoun returns home,' was his response, which under any other circumstances Mary would have rejoiced in, this a further indicator of her father's continued and new-found approval of the man she loved. Yet as matters stood after Cranstoun returned to the house, Mary had to quash her feelings of rage and betrayal until breakfast was finished, though her father did mention, 'You look very pale, Molly; what is the matter with you?' To which Mary replied, 'I am not very well, sir'. Once Mary and Cranstoun were alone, the inevitable scene ensued; Cranstoun must have known the jig was up when Mary presented him with the key to his trunk. And to drive her point home, she 'bade him be more careful for the future, and not leave his letters so much exposed'. According to Mary, on the realisation of his exposure, Cranstoun 'almost fainted away' and immediately made for his own room, presumably to ruminate on how best to wriggle out of his current situation, especially in view of the irrefutable written evidence – he must have kicked himself for having left the key in the lock of his trunk. Understandably upset, Mary went to her own room, but before she could slam the door, Cranstoun appeared and begged her 'for God's sake, to come to him', which, possibly against her better judgement, Mary 'instantly did'. For upwards of two hours a tearful and contrite Cranstoun, on his knees, entreated Mary to forgive him.

While it would be wrong to assume that the Blandy household servants listened at keyholes, human nature being what it is, they might have anticipated that before the day was out there would be one less place to set at the table and one less bed to make each morning. In spite of his pleadings, Mary's resolution nevertheless seemed set firm, and she asked the miserable wretch to make some excuse to leave Henley the following day, and that she, to ameliorate the obvious embarrassment to both parties, would 'not expose you, if I can help it; and our affair may scorn to go off by degrees'. Unless Cranstoun could somehow turn the situation, this looked to be game over, but his hold over Mary was still strong, even in the face of such barefaced infidelity. As Mary turned to leave the room, Cranstoun threw himself onto the bed, crying out, 'I am ruined, I am ruined. Oh Molly, you never loved me!' Resolute and still unmoved by his tearful implorings, Mary made for the door. But the wailing captain clung to her skirts, and swore that 'He would not live till night' if she did not forgive him, adding a measure of emotional blackmail to his last-ditch effort by beseeching her to remember her 'mother's last dying commands, and reflect upon the pain it would give his mother'. Seeing that the doorway into Mary's heart had opened a chink, Cranstoun wedged his foot in, though 'he could never forgive himself', if Mary in the sweetness of her loving forbearance could, then 'he never would repeat the same provocations'. Mary crumbled. Cranstoun had prevailed in his blatant manipulation of her emotions, and for good measure, succeeded in wringing a declaration from Mary that she 'would not break off her acquaintance with him'. After this drama had played itself out, and those servants who might have been eavesdropping had stealthily returned to their domestic chores, Cranstoun conveniently took to his room 'sick' for two or three days until the emotional storm had fully blown over. Though Mary had yielded to his pathetic though obviously convincing performance, she nevertheless, when she later had time to rue events from the condemned cell, recalled that, 'I cannot help thinking this now to have been only a delusion'. If only she had seen through Cranstoun's 'delusion' sooner, she could have saved herself a lot of heartache, as well as her father's life, and imperilling her own 'immortal soul'.

Sometime after the upheaval of the untoward discovery of the London mistress had been smoothed over, Cranstoun received a letter from his brother, Lord Cranstoun, to say that their mother was extremely ill and that he should set out immediately for Nether Crailing as Lady Cranstoun's life was in the balance. As ever, Cranstoun was financially embarrassed, 'Good God, what shall I do! I have no money to carry me thither and all my fortune is seized on, but my half-pay!' Presumably any residue of the loan offered by Mrs Mounteney, freeing Cranstoun from the threat of the bailiffs, had long since been spent. Cranstoun, however, knew he could play Mary like a fiddle – telling her that he would pawn his watch 'in order to enable him to raise a sum sufficient to defray the expense of his journey to Scotland', doubtless if Mary had any ready money of her own she would have given it happily, but as Cranstoun must have predicted, instead she offered to 'freely make him a present of my own watch; as I could not bear to see him [Cranstoun] without one'. Mary did, however, remove the miniature of Cranstoun which she had attached to her watch, as a keepsake. Though in this instance it was Mary's watch that had provided the surety for Cranstoun's travel expenses, in one of the many accounts later penned by her detractors, Mary had supposedly stooped to other nefarious means. It was alleged that she had misdirected an allowance provided by her father, intended to pay for 'mourning for the Prince of Wales' (who had been killed in an accident whilst playing cricket) into Cranstoun's pocket. In the event of a royal death, the populace was expected to dress themselves in sombre attire, especially families with any pretension to gentility, whether or not they had ever attended court. It was also said that on other occasions Mary had funded Cranstoun with money that she had borrowed from her own maid's savings; if this accusation were founded, this would certainly have been seen as an abuse of class privilege.

With the necessary cash now in his hands, after the travel arrangements were made, two days later Cranstoun departed for Scotland, boarding the post-chaise, a closed, four-wheeled coach drawn by a team of fast horses, at six o'clock in the morning, but not before a moving scene of departure was played out with Mary and her father, who had risen especially early to take his leave of the captain. Taking Cranstoun in his arms, and saying 'God bless you, my dear Cranstoun, when you come next, I hope your unhappy affair will be decided to our mutual satisfaction', Cranstoun replied, 'Yes, sir, I hope in my favour; or if this should fail that you should hear of my death. Be tender to and comfort this poor thing', turning towards Mary, 'whom I love better than myself'. In an unaccustomed and overt display of affection, Francis Blandy then embraced them both, and according to Mary's *Own Account* they 'all shed tears'. As the couple bid their final farewells, Mary's father hurried back into the house to fetch a half pint silver dram-bottle, filled with rum, of which he freely made a present to Cranstoun 'bidding him keep the dram-bottle for his sake, and drink the liquor on the road' assuring him that if he found himself 'sick or cold, the latter would prove a cordial to him'. Presumably, the silver dram-bottle later made its way into the pawn shop, while the reciprocal 'gift' that Cranstoun was later to give to Francis, via the hand of his daughter, would certainly prove something less of a 'cordial'.

As the coach departed, Mary waved goodbye until it was lost to view. It was November 1750. Mary would never set eyes on her faithless lover again.

Chapter 5

Messengers of Death

Prior to his final farewell to Henley, to smooth the way for the planned proxy poisoning of Francis Blandy, Cranstoun had been astute enough to lay some manipulative psychological groundwork of a supernatural nature, and one which was to influence the entire Blandy household.

Cranstoun knew that Mary herself was receptive to the idea of spirits returning from beyond the grave, to communicate with the living from the afterlife. According to her *Own Account*, whilst Mary and her mother were staying in London, their conversation had one day turned to 'apparitions' and the 'immortality of the soul'. While the fascination with Spiritualism and psychic phenomena was yet to reach its zenith in the late Victorian era, toward the close of the nineteenth century, middle-class Georgians were nevertheless open to a curiosity and belief in the supernatural. While Anne Blandy's reverend brother would later prove dismissive of such notions, both mother and daughter had made a promise to one another that the first of them to die would appear to the survivor after death 'if permitted so to do'. After Anne Blandy's death in late September of the previous year, Mary had taken to retiring to the room in which her mother had passed away, in the hopes of seeing her wraith. Though Mary carried on this metaphysical experiment for nearly six months, it was to no avail; there were no stirrings from the crypt of St Mary's church and her mother's spirit remained silent. Whether or not Francis Blandy was equally open to paranormal suggestion, he was nonetheless particularly disturbed after one night when he was woken by someone knocking on his chamber door in the early hours. The sound of rustling skirts led him to believe that it was Mary, though she failed to enter when bidden. When the sleep-deprived Francis Blandy had gone into his daughter's room the following morning, demanding to know why she 'had so frighted him', Mary assured her father that she had not set foot outside of her own room all night, yet when the entire household staff were interrogated, he was met with a similar denial.

Capitalising on this nocturnal incident, Cranstoun contrived one morning to appear at breakfast with such a pallid appearance as to give cause for concern. When Mary asked, 'What made him look so pale, and to seem so uneasy?' Cranstoun replied:

> 'I have met with the oddest accident this night that ever befel me: the moment I got into bed, I heard the finest music that can possibly be imagined. I sat up in my bed upon this, to hear from whence it came; and it seemed to me to come from the middle of the stairs. It continued, as I believe, at least above two hours.'

While a house guest at Hart Street, Cranstoun had been lodged in the 'hall-chamber', over the great parlour, reckoned to be the best room in the house, away from the rest of the family rooms. Though Mary laughingly dismissed Cranstoun's account of the ghostly music as 'whimsical', he was to maintain that he really had heard it and that it had been no dream, as 'it began soon after I got into bed'. Mary reassured Cranstoun that 'nothing ill, sure, can be presaged by music', and when her father joined them for breakfast, the subject was hastily dropped. However, the following night, in her own room at the other end of the house, Mary lay awake and listened. She must have been particularly susceptible to the power of Cranstoun's suggestion, as that night she herself heard 'exceedingly plainly' music coming from the direction of the yard. Yet on investigation there seemed to be no earthly explanation. Her mother's old maid, Susannah Gunnell, had an explanation of her own, however; even if Mary was beguiled by the captain's affections, Susannah obviously had the measure of him, and, rather flippantly for one in her menial position, told Mary that 'You see and hear, Madam, with Mr. Cranstoun's eyes and ears'.

Needless to say, accounts of the haunting night-time melody were soon the talk of the household, and latterly the formerly dismissive Susannah Gunnell was to apologetically admit to her mistress that she too had heard a repeat performance herself. At length, and after some discussion, Cranstoun and Mary decided that a nocturnal vigil, including Susannah Gunnell, would resolve the matter, though it was thought sensible not to tell Francis Blandy of their intentions. It was agreed that the hall-chamber would be the best venue, and from Cranstoun's room, at midnight, the trio heard the same music obligingly played out again, but this time some additional, non-instrumental accompaniments were heard. Noises resembling thumping or knocking at a door, followed by footsteps were assumed by Mary to be the tread of her dear deceased mother, on her way downstairs toward the kitchen, the door to which was audibly opened, after which the footsteps were heard to ascend the stairs again. At this point, all three of them were terrified (how much of their fear fed off one another's we can only guess) but Mary, overcoming her uneasiness and taking a rational view of the situation, suggested that 'Surely it must be one of the maids'. Steeling herself to investigate, before she could take up a candle however Cranstoun stopped her, saying 'Perhaps it may be your father, don't let him see you here'; a shrewd intervention on his part as it would have been far beyond the bounds of propriety for Mary to be seen exiting her fiancé's room in the middle of the night. Summoning up his own courage, Cranstoun took it upon himself to open the door. There was nothing to see. Yet when Mary went to return to her own room to get some sleep, it now being past four o'clock in the morning, with her hand on the door handle she perceived that someone, or something, was on the other side. But when the door was opened all that could be discerned were footsteps again descending the back stairs.

Shaken by the episode, Cranstoun and Mary decided to seek some spiritual reassurance and paid a visit to the Reverend Mr Stevens, Anne Blandy's brother, who was the incumbent rector of St Mary the Virgin in the nearby parish of Fawley. Giving her uncle an account of the spectral goings-on at Hart Street, the Reverend Stevens hastily dismissed the mysterious happenings as some trick of the servants, to which Mary's response was that while they might be able to 'make the noise, they could not the music'. The disdainful Reverend Stevens promptly changed the subject.

By now it would seem that all the servants who slept in the main house had heard both the music and the noises; Betty Binfield, the cook-maid, was decidedly rattled by 'such a noise in the room over my master's study', which she described as the tread of a heavy person walking. Of course, there was always the possibility that Cranstoun himself had somehow contrived some or all of the ghostly distractions to further his own end game, as will become clear. He may have even donned a dress himself to rustle at Francis's bedroom door! He knew that for his ploy to work, it would be necessary to induce a widespread state of anxiety throughout the household, and whether or not he was responsible in some measure, or capitalising on coincidence, Cranstoun now started to work on Francis.

Venturing to raise the subject of the haunting melody with Francis, on doing so he was nevertheless met with an attitude equally dismissive as Mary's uncle, her father exclaiming, 'Are you light-headed?' to which Cranstoun responded 'Your daughter, sir, has heard the same, and so have all your servants.' 'It was Scotch music, I suppose' retorted the old man, plainly annoyed by such assertions, yet he must have sat up and taken some notice when, a fortnight before Cranstoun's departure for Scotland, the captain one morning announced that he been visited in the night, as the clock struck two, by the wraith of the old gentleman himself. Dressed 'with his white stockings, his coat on, and a cap on his head' as one would imagine, Francis 'did not seem pleased with the discourse', his fractious response being:

> 'It must have been a dream, for I went to bed at eleven o'clock, and did not rise out of it till seven this morning. Besides, I could not have appeared in my coat, as you pretend, since the maid had it to put a button upon it.'

Feeding the mounting fears of everyone at Hart Street, and playing directly into Cranstoun's hands, Mary exacerbated the household's already suggestible state of moderate hysteria when she mentioned the appearance of her father's apparition to the maids. Expressing her concern that such a vision 'boded no good to her father' Mary elaborated, 'and told how Mr. Cranstoun had learned from a cunning woman in Scotland that they were the messengers of death and that her father would die within the year'. Cranstoun's objective was clear; with the portent of imminent death uppermost on everyone's mind, he had succeeded in setting the stage for Francis Blandy's demise, priming the acceptance of a 'natural' death, free from suspicion, as it had already been foretold.

Cranstoun's ruse was effective in more than influencing Mary and the household staff, however, as Francis's own dismissive behaviour must have belied the fact that he himself had taken the incident to heart. From the time that Cranstoun had apprised him of his apparent visitation, the old attorney's health began to fail. It would have been difficult to ignore the whispering voices which fell silent whenever he entered a room, not to mention the askance looks cast in his direction by his superstitious servants, and the obvious effect on the demeanour of his suggestible daughter.

Francis was now in his sixtieth year (baptised in St Michael & All Angels in Letcombe Bassett on 24 October 1690) and though life expectancy at birth had risen by the late eighteenth century to about forty years old, this of course was an average taken over an entire population, the vast majority of whom would not have enjoyed the comfortable life that he was used to. And indeed, Mary's father had experienced reasonably good health throughout his life, except for his suffering from gout, referred to as the eighteenth century's signature condition, 'the arthritis of the rich', and the 'gravel', another common condition characterised by the formation of small stones in the kidneys, migrating to the bladder and painfully passed when going to the lavatory. Francis also suffered from heartburn, but this was another common enough complaint, familiar today, and often the consequence of dining too well. Though none of these conditions was life-threatening, the symptoms which Francis intermittently suffered must have doubtless been exacerbated by the stress he experienced over the course of his daughter's long and emotionally fraught engagement, not to mention latterly by the supernatural portent of his own death.

It would seem that Francis also experienced some dental problems. A commonplace health issue in the Georgian era with the availability of sugar from the West Indies, for those who could afford it, cases of tooth decay soared in the eighteenth century. William Addis was yet to market the first mass-produced toothbrush, hand-made from pig's bristle, in 1780, but priced at sixpence each they were expensive and often shared! However, as with the other aforementioned medical conditions affecting Mary's father, though of course tooth decay was in no way mortal, his dental health would nevertheless later be construed as a symptom of something far more sinister; at Mary's trial, it was mistakenly assumed by the prosecution, on the grounds of her father losing his teeth, that Francis had begun to manifest the effects of poisoning soon after Cranstoun left Henley in November 1750. As the systematic poisoning of Francis did not commence until the late spring/ early summer of 1751 however, it is likely that prior to this the old man was the victim of nothing more injurious than good old-fashioned dental decay. Even supposing that the powders which Cranstoun had stirred into his tea the previous August had been arsenic, that single dose would not have been sufficient to bring about a marked and sustained deterioration in Francis Blandy's health.

Despite his apparent new-found regard for Cranstoun, demonstrated by his emotional farewell when the captain left for Scotland, in Cranstoun's absence Francis's fickle nature eventually won through, his irascibility possibly worsened by the supposed spectral portents of his death, not to mention the probability of raging toothache! Her father's temper 'much altered for the worse', Mary now found herself frequently upbraided for 'having rejected much better offers than any that had come from Scotland', never mind the fact that it was her father himself who had vetoed the credentials of all those hopefuls who had previously sought her hand, and that her first engagement to that other army captain had been broken off through no fault of her own. At length, Francis ordered his daughter 'to write to Mr. Cranstoun not to return to Henley, till his affair with Miss Murray [Mrs Anne Cranstoun] was quite decided'. The dutiful daughter compiled and communicated her parent's ominous instruction, even though she herself was already aware of what Francis was ignorant; that the appeal had long since been dismissed, and that while his wife lived, Cranstoun could never legally marry Mary.

The contents of Mary's letter must only have served to highlight to Cranstoun what he already knew; that at any time Francis might learn the truth for himself, and in that case, his hopes of getting his hands on Mary's £10,000 dowry would this time be irrevocably dashed. The sands of time were decidedly running against him.

Toward the end of April, or the beginning of May 1751, according to Mary's recollection, she received a letter from Cranstoun telling her that he had seen Mrs Morgan, that cunning woman known to him in Scotland, who held the key to solving all their problems. Confident that he could procure some of her 'powders', he would enclose these along with the 'Scotch pebbles' he intended to send as a gift to Mary. Pieces of jewellery set with Scottish semi-precious hard stones were very popular at the time – 'Ornaments of Scotch pebbles,' to quote Lady Russell, 'were the extreme of fashion in the year 1750'. It is noteworthy that in her reply to Cranstoun, Mary said that she was 'surprised that a man of his sense could believe such efficacy to be lodged in any powder whatsoever', going so far as to say that she would not give it to her father, 'lest it should impair his health'. Cranstoun parried this reluctance by saying in turn 'That he was extremely surprised' Mary should believe he would send anything that might 'prove prejudicial' to her father, particularly 'when his own interest was so apparently concerned in his preservation'. Mary must have guessed that Cranstoun was referring to a conversation between them, shortly before his departure for Scotland, in which she had inferred that though she supposed her father *not* to be a man of a very considerable fortune, nevertheless, if he lived, she was persuaded he would 'provide very handsomely for us and ours, as he lived so retired, and his business was every day increasing'.

Hopeful that Mary's concerns were allayed, Cranstoun went ahead and sent 'some of the aforesaid powder' anyway, enclosed with the Scotch pebbles, in a folded paper upon which were written the words 'powder to clean Scotch pebbles' – his explanation for the misdirection, as stated by Mary, being that 'if he gave it its true name, the box should be opened, and he be laughed at by the person opening it, and taken for a superstitious fool, as he had been by me [Mary] before'. Of course, the 'pebble cleaning powder' was arsenic. Easily obtainable by Cranstoun, and at very little expense to himself, since Medieval times the increase in the number of apothecary shops in many towns and cities meant that any number of toxic substances were easily available and inexpensively so – particularly arsenic. Available in a white oxide powder form derived from the metallic ore, a by-product of an emerging smelting industry, the fatal dose, known to be an amount equivalent in size to a pea, could be purchased for pennies. And the purchase of such potentially lethal substances like arsenic, and mercury for that matter, were at the time unrestricted, and usually went unquestioned as a popular use for arsenic was as a pesticide, specifically used to kill rats, while mercury was used to control body lice. But of course, either substance could be employed for more malign purposes. After all, as Alfred Swaine Taylor, the famed nineteenth century toxicologist is quoted as saying 'A poison in a small dose is a medicine, a medicine in a large dose is a poison'.

The poison of popular choice then, the murderous use of arsenic became so widespread that in France arsenic came to be known as *Poudre de succession*, 'inheritance powder' and eventually because of the number of murder cases involving arsenic in Britain, the government was forced to introduce in 1851 the 'Arsenic Act' forbidding the sale of any arsenic compounds to a purchaser who was unknown to the supplying pharmacist or apothecary. Would-be poisoners were further thwarted by the introduction of a requirement that all manufacturers of arsenic powder mix one ounce of a colouring agent (indigo or soot were usually employed) to every pound of arsenic powder produced, though the introduction of these precautions was cold comfort to all those earlier victims who had already succumbed to the hand of the poisoner. Although many poisons were readily available, statistics show that arsenic alone accounted for nearly half of the poisoning cases brought before English courts between 1750 and 1914, arsenical poisoning attributed to 237 of those 504 criminal cases to be precise, though of course, this figure does not include those cases of poisoners never brought before a court, evading prosecution. Small wonder then that by the 1830s, morbid descriptions of murders with arsenic terrified the public and became a staple of the British popular press.

In the poisoning of Francis Blandy, there does, however, seem to be some dispute as to when the first of the fatal doses was administered. According to the opening speech for the Crown at her trial, Mary received the first of the powders, mailed to her by Cranstoun along with the Scotch pebbles, in the April of 1751; in her *Own Account*, however, Mary says they did not reach her hands until June. According to the witness testimony of Susannah Gunnell, the maidservant who had taken part in the ghostly midnight vigil, she remembered two consignments of 'pebbles' arriving in Henley from

Scotland, one 'in a large box of table linen,' which came 'early in the spring,' the second in 'a small box' some three months before her master's death, that presumably being sometime in May, Francis Blandy dying on 14 August.

Whenever they arrived, along with the fatal consignments Cranstoun had enclosed instructions 'to mix the powder in tea', and according to Mary, 'This some mornings after I did'. While it was noted that the earlier phase of Francis's fatal 'illness' began to manifest in June, as the symptoms of chronic arsenic poisoning develop after repeated minor exposure to the toxic element, emerging gradually, often with remissions and recurrences as the poison accumulates in the body, it is difficult to pinpoint when Mary served her father's first cup of 'powder' laced tea. It is the cumulative effect of arsenic, when administered in small doses, over a span of time, which causes death once the critical level is reached, and as a consequence, the time it takes for a victim to die is largely in the hands of the poisoner. However, in Francis's case it was a larger final dose which brought about his death.

Though Mary was to complain to Cranstoun that she found the powder 'would not mix well with tea' certainly sufficient repeated doses must have been ingested by her father who 'suffered much internal pain and frequently was sick'. Tellingly, others in the Blandy household were to suffer similar symptoms. It was a foible of Mary's father that he was in the habit of having his tea served 'in a different dish from the rest of the family'. The earliest tea cups had no handles and were referred to as tea bowls or 'dishes'. One morning, Susannah Gunnell, on clearing away the breakfast things, on finding that her master's tea had been left virtually untouched, drank the brew herself. For three days after she was violently sick, and continued to feel unwell for a week. On another occasion, when Francis again left his morning tea undrunk, rather than see it go to waste, it was offered to an old charwoman, Ann Emmet, who was often employed about the house. Whether she drank more freely than Susannah, or perhaps the cup contained a greater dose, shortly afterwards she was seized with a 'sickness so severe as to endanger her life'. As Mary was now mistress of the house, and in charge of domestic matters, she would have been well aware of both these instances, and in the case of the old charwoman she was concerned enough to send white wine, whey, and broth to speed her recovery.

While Mary could not have been blind to these coincidental circumstances, she nevertheless carried on dosing her father. When she had mentioned to Cranstoun the difficulty of the powders not mixing 'well with tea', she also noted that on 'looking into the cup, I saw nothing adhere to the sides of it; nor was such an adhesion probable, as the powder swam on the top of the liquor'. Though arsenic presented itself as the ideal poison because it was colourless and tasteless, its insolubility was a dead giveaway. While it could be dispersed in a hot beverage, once the liquid started to cool precipitate particles were noticeable. Indeed, this was an observation which would later form part of the criteria for one of the toxicological tests performed by Dr Addington in proving that the powders were, in fact, arsenic, but here we jump ahead of Mary's story. Writing to Cranstoun of the problems she was experiencing, that the tea was an unsuitable medium for administering the powders, Cranstoun nevertheless had a ready answer. He wrote to Mary on 18 July, 'I am sorry there are such occasions to clean your pebbles; you must make use of the powder to them by putting it in anything of substance wherein it will not swim a–top of the water'. Though the language was guarded, any direct reference to the true nature of the 'pebble cleaning' powders disguised in case his letter be read by a third party, the suggestion was clear. A more substantial method of delivery was required. And the solution was to present itself in one of Francis's favourite foods – gruel. A common dish at the time, gruel was a thinner version of porridge, usually made by boiling oats in water or milk, which could be drunk as well as eaten. Gruel then would prove just the thing 'of substance' for the powders to be mixed with.

In the same letter, Cranstoun also took the opportunity to include some further encouragement in the hopes of hastening Mary toward their ultimate goal, with his descriptions of the beauties of Scotland, and letting drop that his mother, Lady Cranstoun, was having an apartment specially fitted up at Lennel House for Mary's use. Pointedly there was no reference to that lady's miraculous recovery, she having been so recently near death, and the reason for Cranstoun's mercy dash north of the border. One has to question whether Lady Cranstoun was ever ill at all, or if her critical condition was an invention on Cranstoun's part to cleverly engineer his absence from Henley while Mary systematically poisoned her father.

On the evening of Sunday, 4 August, Mary instructed Susannah to make up a pan of 'water gruel' for her father, a usual enough request. At noon on the following day, Mary was seen in the pantry by the kitchen staff, stirring the pan of gruel herself with a spoon, remarking that she had been eating the oatmeal from the bottom of the pot. Whether or not she was putting on a pre-emptive show of confidence by freely eating the gruel herself, or merely satisfying a lunchtime hunger pang, her next action was decidedly suspicious. 'Taking some up in the spoon, [she] put it between her fingers and rubbed it.' That evening some of the same gruel was sent up in a half-pint mug on Mary's orders for her father's supper. However, before the dish left the kitchen, Mary was again seen repeating her curious actions of earlier that day, taking a little of the gruel on a spoon and rubbing it between her fingers.

Clearly, the consistency of her father's favourite food had enabled Mary to incorporate a larger dose of the powders undetected as, by the following morning, Tuesday, the Hart Street household was in an uproar, Francis having been taken seriously ill in the night. Tellingly, the absorption of arsenic is dependent on how it is administered. In a suspension, such as in tea, the poison is absorbed very rapidly, but as previously mentioned, due to its precipitative nature and the risk of detection, the size of the dose is necessarily limited. However, in a larger dose administered in a powdered form incorporated in a semi-solid, though it is more readily eliminated from the body, what remains in the stomach and intestines can literally scour the internal membranes, causing inflammation which, over the course of hours can result in ulceration to the point where internal perforation develops. When Mr Norton, the Henley apothecary, was hastily called in; he was not a trained physician, though many sought the services of an apothecary when taken ill, technically their role was that of a 'medical retailer', he diagnosed his patient's violent pain, vomiting, and purging, to the best of his ability, as 'a fit of colic'. This was a reasonable enough assumption, as the symptoms of abdominal colic can mirror those of acute arsenic poisoning, and at this point there was no reason to suspect that anything more malevolent was at play.

When Norton questioned Francis as to whether or not he had eaten anything which might have disagreed with him, Mary, who was present in her father's bedroom at the time, replied 'that her papa had had nothing that she knew of, except some peas on the Saturday night before'. No mention was made of gruel. But then on the face of it this was an innocuous, bland enough dish, and Mary was hardly likely to reference it as a possible cause of her father's ill health. Administering some remedies from his apothecary bag, Norton said he would call again the following day, with a further prescription in case the symptoms had not abated.

That evening, Mary asked Susannah to warm some of the remaining gruel left in the pot for her father's supper, which Mary took and served herself. Did she perhaps take this opportunity to add a little, or a lot more of the powders into this particular helping? A distinct possibility, as by the time Francis retired to bed, he was vomiting repeatedly, and Susannah had to hurry him a basin.

The next morning, the remains of Francis's partially eaten supper was brought down from his room, and the leftovers offered by Betty Binfield, the

'Miss Mary Blandy in her Drawing Room' - Mezzotint by T Ryley

Henley-on-Thames seen from the Wargrave Road
A bucolic view of Henley painted by the Flemish landscape artist Jan Siberechts in 1698.

Blandy House, Hart Street, Henley-on-Thames

Mary grew up in the Blandy's family mansion on Hart Street, surrounded by lovely gardens, close to the Thames. (Hart Street, the road from Henley Bridge to the crossroads, takes its name from the fifteenth-century White Hart Inn on the street's north side. It is now a restaurant.)

(Image courtesy of Philip Bell, taken from Mr Bell's Travels*)*

Henley Bridge, engraved by Frederick Hay from a drawing by John Preston Neale
Taken from *The Beauties of England and Wales, 1812.*

St Mary the Virgin, Henley's Parish Church

The church's historic records hold an entry for the marriage of Mary's parents, Francis Blandy and Anne Stevens, dated 22 September 1719. While the exact date of Mary's birth is not known, the church records for the year 1720 do yield details of her baptism, that 'Mary, of Fransis' [sic] was christened on 15 July. (As a general rule, English parish registers recorded dates of baptisms rather than births, the average age at baptism increasing from one week old in the middle of the seventeenth century, to one month by the middle of the nineteenth century.) *(Image courtesy of Philip Bell, taken from* Mr Bell's Travels*)*

Interior of St Mary the Virgin, Henley

After her execution, Mary's body was returned to Henley for burial and was interred in the chancel of St Mary's, between the graves of her father and her mother. As the church has since undergone restoration there is now no indication of the Blandy family grave, however it is believed to be located beneath the organ in the north choir aisle. *(Image courtesy of Russ Hamer)*

View of Bath in the eighteenth century - Engraving by W Elliott after T Robins
As the local pool of eligible suitors in the environs of Henley-on-Thames seemed distinctly shallow, the Blandys decamped to Bath for the season, which was then acknowledged as the great matrimonial marketplace, in the hopes of securing a suitable husband for Mary.
(Courtesy of Wellcome Images)

Sack-back gown, 1775-1780
In the eighteenth century appearance was everything. The 'sack back' dress, which had become increasingly fashionable in the 1730s and would remain so until the 1780s, required a considerable amount of costly fabric, and was an overt display of the wearer's wealth and social standing. *(Image courtesy of the V&A Museum)*

Captain William Henry Cranstoun - from an Engraving by B Cole.

Cranstoun presented himself as perfect husband material, on paper at least… A younger son of the fifth Lord Cranstoun, his Scottish pedigree impressed Mary's socially aspiring parents, even though his house was somewhat fiscally embarrassed, and he had little more than his army pay to support himself. According to a contemporary account of his physical appearance: 'In his person he is remarkably ordinary, his stature is low, his face freckled and pitted with the smallpox, his eyes small and weak, his eyebrows sandy, and his shape no ways genteel; his legs are clumsy, and he has nothing in the least elegant in his manner.' Yet something about Cranstoun must have appealed to Mary.

Cap: WILLIAM HENRY CRANSTOUN
With his Funeral Procession in Flanders.

Park Place, from an old print - *Anne Seymour Damer: A Woman of Art and Fashion, 1748-1828*

Long since a favourite trysting spot while Mary and Cranstoun were courting, the couple would hold their assignations in the grounds surrounding this opulent Palladian mansion, just across the Thames in Remenham. The location where they often met later became romantically known as 'Miss Blandy's Walk'.

John Bowles's view of St. James's Square, London c.1752
Mrs Pocock's London residence in St James's Square was to prove a convenient meeting place for Mary and Cranstoun while they were both in town. A very good friend of Mary's mother, Mrs Pocock obligingly put her home at the disposal of the lovers after Mary's uncle made it clear that Cranstoun was not a welcome guest in his London home.

Georgian porcelain tea 'dish' and saucer
It was a foible of Francis Blandy's that he was in the habit of having his tea served 'in a different dish from the rest of the family.' When clearing away the breakfast things one morning, the maid, Susannah Gunnell, found that her master's tea had been left untouched and so drank the brew herself; she was violently sick for three days afterwards and continued to feel unwell for a week thereafter.

The Little Angel, Remenham

After escaping her house arrest, Mary was pursued by a mob of enraged townsfolk over the Henley bridge into Remenham, where the landlady of the now famous 'Little Angel', Mrs Davis, allowed her to take refuge before being taken back into custody. *(Image courtesy of The Little Angel Pub Henley.)*

Entrance to Calais Harbour, **watercolour by David Cox, c.1829**

As soon as Cranstoun got wind of Mary's likely arrest, he fled the country. On 4 September 1751 he embarked on a 'packet ship' bound for Calais, and went into hiding, out of the reach of the British authorities.

Mary Blandy taking tea in Oxford Gaol

In the weeks leading up to her trial, the conditions of Mary's imprisonment were described as 'indeed rather like a retirement from the world than the confinement of a criminal'. With her maid to attend her and the best rooms in the Keeper's house at her disposal, Mary took tea twice daily - amongst the personal items she was allowed to take with her to gaol was her tea chest, its canisters 'all most full of fine Hyson'. *(Image taken from* Portraits, memoirs, and characters, of remarkable persons, from the revolution in 1688 to the end of the reign of George II. Collected from the most authentic accounts extant, *(1820)*

MISS MOLLY BLANDY
who with her own & her Sweethearts Contrivance did Barbarously and Inhumanly Poison her own Father for his Estate.

Mary (Molly) Blandy before her execution, 1752

On her arrival at Oxford Gaol, Mary's first question was, 'Am I to be fettered?' She was told that she would not be put into leg irons, so long as she behaved well. However, when a rumour reached the authorities in London that a plan was afoot to break Mary out of gaol, her fears of being 'fettered' were realised. In this image the leg irons are visible above Mary's stylish shoes. *(Courtesy of Wellcome Images)*

Close up of the leg iron seen around Mary's ankle in the previous image.

A pair of old iron 'leg bracelets' similar to those riveted about Mary's dainty ankles.

(Image courtesy of André Karwath)

Divinity Hall, Oxford - **Engraving by D Loggan**

The venue for Mary's trial. As the Town Hall, where the Oxford Assizes were usually held, was being refurbished at the time, and as the University authorities had refused the use of the Sheldonian Theatre (the official ceremonial hall of the University of Oxford), the hall of the Divinity School was chosen instead. The date of the trial was set for Tuesday, 3 March 1752. *(Image courtesy of The Wellcome Trust)*

Portrait of Henry Bathurst, 2nd Earl Bathurst c.1776

Appearing for the Crown, the Honourable Mr Bathurst led the prosecution at Mary's trial. Bathurst was later destined to rise to the office of Lord Chancellor. However, even though he was promoted to the highest judicial office, he has been described as 'the least efficient Lord Chancellor of the eighteenth century'.

Bust of Dr Anthony Addington by Thomas Banks

Mary Blandy's case was notable in that it was the first time that detailed medical evidence had been presented in a court of law on a charge of murder by poisoning, and the first time that any court had accepted toxicological evidence in an arsenic poisoning case. It was to be the making of Dr Anthony Addington's career, who appeared as expert witness for the prosecution. *(Image courtesy of Jonathan Cardy, photographed with the permission of the V&A Museum)*

Chemist's laboratory, 1760

Dr Addington's skills as a chemist proved that Francis Blandy had ingested arsenic, a poison formerly considered undetectable. Though rudimentary by today's standards, he was nevertheless able to convince the court on the basis of his tests that the powder Mary had put in her father's food and drink was indeed arsenic, regardless of her 'intention' to do so. *(Image courtesy of The Wellcome Trust)*

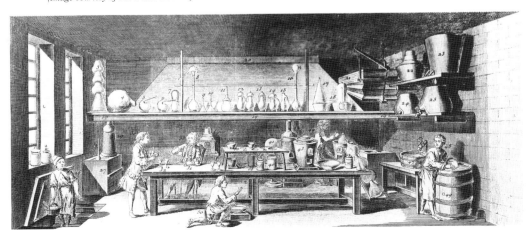

THE

TRYAL

OF

MARY BLANDY, *Spinster*;

FOR

The MURDER of her *FATHER*,

FRANCIS BLANDY, *Gent.*

At the ASSIZES held at *Oxford*
For the COUNTY of *Oxford*,

On SATURDAY the 29th of FEBRUARY, 1752.

BEFORE

The Honourable HENEAGE LEGGE, *Esq*;
AND
Sir SYDNEY STAFFORD SMYTHE, *Knt.*

Two of the BARONS of his MAJESTY's Court of EXCHEQUER.

Publiſhed by Permiſſion of the Judges.

LONDON:

Printed for JOHN and JAMES RIVINGTON, at the *Bible* and *Crown*, in St. *Paul's Church-Yard.* M. DCC. LII.

[Price TWO SHILLINGS.]

Frontispiece to '*The tryal of Mary Blandy, spinster: for the murder of her father, Francis Blandy, gent., at the assizes held at Oxford for the county of Oxford, on Saturday the 29th of February, 1752 : before the Honourable Heneage Legge, esq; and Sir Sydney Stafford Smythe, knt., two of the barons of His Majesty's Court of exchequer. Published by permission of the judges*'

This rather long-winded title was just one of many such publications to appear in the wake of Mary's conviction. Horace Bleackley, one of Mary's biographers writing in 1905, listed in his bibliography no less than thirty 'contemporary tracts' pertaining to the Mary Blandy case. (See Appendix) *(Courtesy of the U.S. National Library of Medicine)*

Capt. CRANSTOUN's
A C C O U N T

Of the poisoning the

Late Mr. FRANCIS BLANDY,

O F

Henley upon Thames, Oxfordshire :

Declared folemnly by him before he died, at *Furnes*, in *Flanders*, on the 30th of *November* laft.

In which are contained

Some Particulars of his private Marriage with the late unfortunate Mifs *Blandy*; and Copies of three Let-ters from the faid Mifs *Blandy*, to him in *Northumber-land*, bearing the feveral Dates of *June* 30, *July* 16, and *Auguft* 1, 1751; which was juft preceding the poifoning of the faid Mr. *Blandy*, which fets that whole tragical Affair in a true Light.

W I T H A N

Account of Mr. *Cranftoun*'s Diftreffes, from the Time he abfconded to his Death, which was attended with the moft terrible Agonies : And in which Part is inferted a Narrative of fome artful and crafty Villanies committed by the fa-mous, or more properly, infamous Capt. P———w, in *France* and *Flanders*, while Mr. *Cranftoun* was in thofe Coun-tries.

The whole publifhed for the Satisfaction of the Public.

L O N D O N:

Printed for R. RICHARDS, the Corner of *Bernard's-Inn*, near the *Black Swan*, *Holborn*.

Front page of the pamphlet entitled: *Capt. Cranstoun's account of the poisoning [of]
the late Mr. Francis Blandy*
Intended as a counterblast to Mary's *Own Account*, incredibly Cranstoun was not
without his apologists. This pamphlet, appearing after Mary's execution, professed to
be Cranstoun's own account, which conveniently 'set that whole tragical Affair in a true
Light'. *(Courtesy of the U.S. National Library of Medicine)*

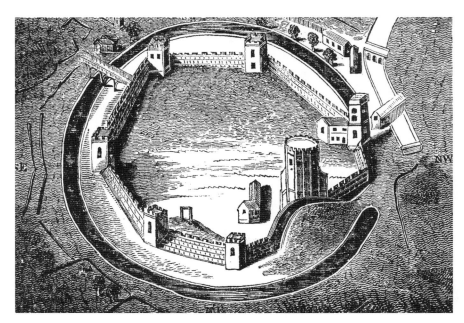

Ancient Plan of Oxford Castle - *The Mirror of Literature, Amusement, and Instruction, Vol. 12, 1828*

The Castle gallows can be seen towards the bottom of the image. They were clearly no longer in use when it came to Mary's execution, in view of the improvised gallows she was hanged from (see next image).

Detail from a contemporary engraving by Benjamin Cole - *Miss Mary Blandy, with scene of her Execution*

There seems to be some confusion as to *where* Mary was hanged. There were two places set aside for public executions at Oxford in the eighteenth century. Hangings would take place either in the Castle Yard (as shown below), or at the gallows set up on a raised mound just outside the West Gate of the city. While contemporary evidence would suggest the former, the depiction on the following page shows the gallows set up outside the West Gate, the site now occupied by the recently redeveloped Westgate shopping centre.

Miss MARY BLANDY

B. Cole Sculp.

Aged 33 and Executed at OXFORD April 6, 1752, for poisoning her Father.

'The Execution of Miss Mary Blandy, for the murder of her father, near Oxford on 6th April 1752, with the Rev. Swinton in attendance.'

(Courtesy of Wellcome Images)

MISS BLANDY *at the place of Execution near Oxford, attended by the Rev^d. M^r. Swinton*

High Street, Oxford - painting by Thomas Malton the Younger

Eager to capitalise on the popularity and fascination stirred up by such high-profile cases as Mary's, publishers and printers profited from the increasing sales of books and pamphlets, especially after her execution. One such was *A Genuine and Impartial Account Of the Life of Miss Mary Blandy*, available from the Oxford bookseller W. Jackson on 'the High', as Oxford's High Street is known, priced at 6d.

The Red Lion Hotel, Henley
Accounts of Mary's hauntings abound, her ghost especially favouring the environs of her old home at Henley-on-Thames, including an appearance at the Red Lion Hotel, on Hart Street, a short distance from the old Blandy family residence. When the night porter saw her wraith standing by a window, he drew a picture so that he wouldn't forget what the apparition looked like. *(Image courtesy of Philip Bell, taken from* Mr Bell's Travels*)*

Dolesden Lane, Turville
The lanes around Turville and Hambleden also seem to be a favourite haunt of Mary's. There have been various sightings of the 'ghost' of a woman in 'old-fashioned clothes' seen on Dolesden Lane, near Turville Court, the home of her mother's good friend Mrs Pocock, and where Mary spent time as a house guest. When seen in this vicinity, witnesses have noted that her dress 'rustles' as she passes by.

cook, to the old charlady Ann Emmet, who happened to be in the kitchen at the time. Though she had clearly recovered from her last bout of sickness after drinking the fateful cup of tea, this time, after finishing off the cold gruel she became violently ill, with symptoms mirroring those of Francis. In fact, her constitution was so affected that even by the following spring she was still too debilitated to attend Mary's trial. When Susannah went upstairs at 9 o'clock to dress her mistress, she mentioned to Mary that Ann had taken another, more serious turn for the worse. To this Mary replied that she was relieved that she had not been downstairs already, 'as it would have shocked her to see "her poor dame" so ill'; an expression of concern tainted with a pang of guilt perhaps?

Later that morning, as promised Norton called again, and to his relief found his patient a little easier. But the respite was to be brief. In the afternoon, Mary told Susannah that as Mr Blandy had taken some 'physic' (medication) he would need some more gruel, presumably to settle the old man's stomach! As Susannah was busy ironing, and as there was still some gruel left in the pot, Mary told her she need not worry to make up any fresh. However, the maid pointed out that the gruel was now stale, being then four days old, and besides, after having tasted a small amount of it herself, Susannah had felt very unwell afterwards. To this Mary pointedly made no comment, but she did warn the cook that if Susannah were to taste anymore from the pot 'she might do for herself—a person of her age'. We can assume that Susannah must have been of advancing years, an old family retainer she had after all been Mrs Blandy's personal maid before her mistress died. It must be questioned whether Mary was concerned for Susannah's well-being, or keen to avoid arousing any further suspicion with regard to the tainted gruel.

While the servants in the Blandy household might have been socially inferior, they certainly were not stupid. Even if the recent and obviously connected occurrences of ill health had apparently failed to arouse the concerns of their mistress, the circumstances were enough to prompt the kitchen maids to take a closer look at the remains of the gruel pan for themselves. Their inspection revealed a white, gritty 'settlement' found at the bottom of the pot. Persuasive of foul play, rather than disposing of the stale contents, it was decided amongst them that the pan should be locked in a cupboard overnight, and the next day, Thursday, wise old Susannah took the pan, along with the suspicions of the kitchen staff, to Mrs Mounteney, the neighbour and longtime friend of Mrs Blandy, who had stood as godmother to Mary. Once acquainted with the facts, and the evidence of the gruel pot, Mrs Mounteney wasted no time in summoning Norton for his opinion. While he must have been familiar with the circumstance of accidental incorporation of arsenic into foodstuffs, it often being mistaken for sugar or flour or cream of tartar, a consequence of careless storage and labelling, the apothecary nevertheless prudently removed the pan's contents, the subsequent analysis of which would later prove to be integral in Mary's prosecution.

Chapter 6

Those Cursed Scotch Pebbles...

The day following Susannah Gunnell's hurry through the streets of Henley with a pot of stale, yet potentially fatal gruel, Mary's uncle, the Reverend Stevens, having received word of his brother-in-law's state of health, called at Hart Street on the morning of Friday 9 August.

On his arrival, Susannah took it upon herself to relate to the Reverend the suspicious circumstances of Francis's illness, and those of the others who had been taken unwell in the household. His counsel was that Susannah should tell her master all that she knew.

She must have tossed and turned in her sleep at the prospect of revealing such a damning supposition, implicating the daughter of the house, as at seven o'clock the following Saturday morning Susannah steeled herself and knocked on her master's bedroom door. She told him of her concerns, and in view of the circumstantial evidence, that his recent illness was suspected of being the result of poison.

After he had recovered from the initial shock, his first question was where did Susannah think Mary could have obtained the poison from, never mind the fact that his daughter had supposedly tried to poison him in the first place! Susannah could only answer that as far as she was concerned, the source was Cranstoun. It did not take long for the penny to drop, and on realising the intent of 'that villain', Francis bemoaned the fact 'that ever he came to my house, eat of the best, drink of the best that my house could afford—to take away my life, and ruin my daughter!' True to form, he prioritised his pecuniary misgivings above those of the attempt on his own life and that of his daughter's wrecked prospects, never mind that she had been systematically poisoning him. Susannah also told him that Norton had been told of the matter and that he had recommended all of Miss Blandy's papers be seized immediately. But to this the old man would not agree, maintaining that 'I never in all my life read a letter that came to my daughter'. He did, however, urge that any remaining 'powders' should be found and secured.

Obviously, Francis wanted to hear what his daughter had to say in the matter. He immediately rose and went downstairs where he found Mary already at breakfast, joined that morning by Robert Littleton, a clerk employed in the Blandy law practice, who had only just returned the night before from a holiday in Warwickshire. When Francis entered the breakfast-parlour, Littleton must have been shocked by the appearance of his employer, whom he took to be in a state of 'great agony' of which he 'complained very much'. At this point, Mary was still unaware that her father had been acquainted with any notion of the suspicion that she had been presumably poisoning him, and handed him his tea, as usual, served in his 'particular dish'. On tasting it, her father firmly fixed his gaze on Mary, and remarked that it had 'a bad, gritty taste', and asked if she had put anything into it? '... too much of the black stuff?' referring to the leaves of Bohea tea habitually served at breakfast in the Blandy household. The colour drained from Mary's face, and in a trembling whisper, she said that 'it was made as usual' before hurrying from the room. Francis promptly tipped away his tea into the 'cat's basin' (a slop bowl) and rang for a fresh cup.

After breakfast, Mary discreetly intercepted Robert Littleton and tellingly asked him whether or not her father had finished his tea. On being told it had been disposed of, she appeared to Littleton 'much upset'. Unless she absented herself from the house, a further confrontation with her father was unavoidable, and when their paths crossed in the kitchen later that morning, in the presence of the cook Betty Binfield, Francis tersely said, 'I had like to have been poisoned once,' adding that:

> 'It was on this same day, the tenth of August, at the coffee-house or at the Lyon [the Red Lion, one of Henley's oldest coaching inns], and two other gentlemen were like to have been poisoned by what they drank.'

Mary began to say that she remembered the incident very well, but was interrupted by her father's interjection that 'One of these gentlemen died immediately, the other is dead now, I have survived them both, and it is my fortune to be poisoned at last'. At length, he turned his hard gaze away from his daughter and left the kitchen.

In a state of inner turmoil, Mary immediately went to her room and gathered together all of the letters she had received from Cranstoun, along with what remained of the powders he had sent her. Certainly, though Francis's scruples concerning the privacy of his daughter's correspondence were admirable, they were, in hindsight, to prove misguided, but then prior to Susannah's devastating revelation, he had no reason to presume that Mary was anything other than a dutiful, loving daughter. Returning to the kitchen, Mary threw the letters and the paper packet containing the powder into the fire grate and 'stirred it down with a stick'. At that moment, whether by chance or design, Betty proceeded to pile some fresh coals onto the kitchen fire, which damped down the flames, and as soon as Mary had left the kitchen, the maids, all things considered now alert to the poisonous accusations, hastily removed the coals. Though each of the letters had been reduced to ash, the folded paper packet still containing an amount of the powder was virtually without a scorch mark, and written thereon, clearly visible in Cranstoun's handwriting were the words, 'The powder to clean the pebbles with'. The packet and its contents were given over to Mr Norton, who when he called at the house later that day found that the condition of his patient had deteriorated. In the circumstances, Mary agreed to the apothecary's suggestion that Dr Anthony Addington should be summoned from Reading.

Addington's services came highly recommended, though it would be his involvement in the Blandy case which would make his name, assuring his professional recognition, in view of his significant contribution toward the acceptance of forensic chemistry to a criminal investigation. Addington was later to include among his eminent patients 'Mad King George', Lord Chatham, better known as William Pitt the Elder, and his son William Pitt the Younger who became the country's youngest Prime Minister. It was the younger Pitt whom Addington had apparently restored to health after prescribing a course of treatment that included a bottle of port wine daily to alleviate his gout! The youngest son of a Berkshire gentleman who held a moderately sized estate at Twyford, Addington would himself go on to father a future Prime Minister, his son Henry Addington holding office between 1801 and 1804, and later created 1st Viscount Sidmouth. Educated, as a commoner, at Winchester School, Addington progressed to Trinity College, Oxford, where he took his MA degree in 1740 and his MD in 1744. Having fixed on medicine as his profession he settled as a physician in Reading. While his was a general practice, Addington gained a particular reputation for the treatment of mental disease. Prior to George III being hampered by his own mental health problems, the king had suggested that Lord Chatham, who had long suffered from bouts of depression, seek another physician to assist Addington with his treatment. Chatham, however, declined the king's suggestion, and ascribed his recovery, from what fellow politicians inferred was 'insanity', to Dr Addington's 'judicious sagacity and kind care'. Though the last two decades of George III's reign were patterned by repeated periods of 'madness' and remission which eventually proved to be unremitting, in 1788, when Addington was called in by the Prince of Wales to attend on his father in his first instance of mental instability, when subsequently examined by a parliamentary committee on the King's condition, Addington alone foretold the early recovery of the King – which did follow – on the grounds he had never known a case of insanity not preceded by melancholy which was not cured within twelve months. Specialising in what would later be recognised as the field of psychology, Addington was to add adjoining premises to his home and surgery specifically for the reception of 'insane patients'. At the time such establishments, presided over by 'mad-doctors' as they came to be called, proved profitable enterprises as there were scant alternatives for the treatment of the insane, and in meeting the demands of patients' families, 'madhouses' like Addington's in Reading were to be the foundation of many a family fortune, and in his case, assist in his rise to the position of court physician, not to mention financially underwriting his son's parliamentary career. Yet it was the considerable public attention which Addington garnered when he appeared as an expert witness for the prosecution at Mary Blandy's trial which did much to assure his later success, as well as, of course, in contributing toward Mary's conviction.

While it was the apothecary Mr Norton who had first suggested that Addington be called in to attend upon her father in his fast-declining state, in her *Own Account* Mary took the full credit for calling in the doctor; perhaps even at this late stage, whether or not she acknowledged to herself the possibility that she had in fact been dosing her own father with poison, perhaps she hoped that the eminent physician would be able to save Francis's life. Her detractors, however, would later say that this was merely a ploy on her part, another attempt to demonstrate her innocence.

It was midnight before Addington arrived. Though the journey from his house in London Street, Reading, to the Blandy's front door was little more than ten miles, over the Caversham Bridge and up the old Henley Road, it would have taken time for the initial summons to reach him, and he may well have been occupied with another case. When he arrived at Hart Street, prior to examining his patient, Addington asked some necessary, if indelicate questions to gain a clearer background to the case. Francis told him that after drinking some gruel on 5 August he had noticed an unusual grittiness in his mouth, a very painful burning and pricking sensation on his tongue and in his throat, that he suffered pain in his stomach and bowels and that he had been subject to fits of vomiting and purging – diarrhoea – thereafter. On examination, it was found that as a result of the repeated purging, the area around Francis's anus had begun to ulcerate, uncomfortable indeed. After taking into account the condition of his patient, and from the additional circumstances that Norton had told him about Addington was left in no doubt; Francis Blandy was suffering from the deleterious effects of poison, presumably deliberately administered.

The doctor at once informed Mary of what she must have already, by now, feared. It would seem improbable that at this stage she could still maintain any belief in Cranstoun's assertions that the powders he had supplied were indeed harmless. When Addington enquired if her father had any enemies, Mary replied 'It is impossible! He is at peace with all the world and all the world is at peace with him'. She did, however, add that her father had long suffered from colic and heartburn, to which his present indisposition must surely be attributable – an act of self-denial on Mary's part, or a shrewd attempt to deflect the truth?

Remaining in the sick room until the following morning, a Sunday, Addington promised to return the next day. It is unlikely that Mary was aware that when he left, the doctor carried with him in his bag the sediment judiciously rescued from the bottom of the gruel pan, along with the packet of powder plucked from the kitchen fire, both of which had been entrusted to Norton's safe keeping. While at this time neither physician or apothecary knew precisely what the powder was, experience and common sense led to their fair assumption that the substance was arsenic. Before he took his leave, Addington confided in Mary that if her father were to die, she would 'inevitably be ruined'.

Mary wasted no time in warning her faithless lover of the severity of the situation that she, and by association, he himself, now found themselves in. Penning a hasty letter addressed to Cranstoun at Lennel House, Coldstream, Mary asked her father's clerk Robert Littleton, who had been in the habit of directing her letters to Cranstoun, to seal, address, and post the letter as usual on her behalf. Clearly, Littleton did not share Francis's scruples with regards to acquainting himself with the contents of another's private correspondence, or perhaps in the circumstances, he felt his transgression was warranted. Unfolding the letter, Littleton read the following:

'Dear Willy, – My father is so bad that I have only time to tell you that if you do not hear from me soon again, don't be frightened. I am better myself. Lest any accident should happen to your letters, take care what you write. My sincere compliments. I am ever yours.'

Littleton at once showed the letter to Norton, who in turn read it aloud to Francis Blandy. Though he must have been aware that he was dying, and by the hand of his own daughter, 'He said very little. He smiled and said, "Poor love-sick girl! What won't a girl do for a man she loves?"' Tearfully adding that 'I forgive her—I always thought there was mischief in those cursed Scotch pebbles'.

Clearly, Mary's paternal uncle, Charles Blandy of Kingston, who had come to visit his ailing brother, thought differently. It was he who decided that in the circumstances it would be prudent to forbid Mary any further access to her father's sick room. This edict was circumvented however the following Monday morning when Francis sent a message, via Susannah, to his daughter 'that he was ready to forgive her if she would but endeavour to bring that villain [Cranstoun] to justice'. In accordance with his dying request, for it was obvious that the end was now near, Mary was admitted to his room one last time, though Susannah and Norton were present throughout.

At this point, Mary was still unaware that the packet of powder she supposed had been destroyed in the kitchen fire had been retrieved intact, and that the contents of her unsent missive to Cranstoun had been read. Initially thinking she was clear of any implication, on being informed of the discovery of such damning evidence, Mary fell to her knees at her father's bedside, and implored his forgiveness, vowing that she would never again see or write to Cranstoun. Too little, too late. While her father granted his forgiveness, he added that he hoped that God would be equally forgiving, as Mary should have 'considered better than to have attempted anything against thy father'. Though the game was up, Mary insisted that for her part she was 'entirely innocent' of causing her father's fatal illness, and while she admitted to having put the powder into his gruel, that 'it was given me with another intent'. It was on this assertion that her later defence was to rest.

In a final show of magnanimity and paternal affection, Francis urged his daughter to leave his sickroom, in case she should accidentally let fall any comment which would ultimately be to her 'own prejudice'. A lawyer to the last. Though he must have entertained no doubt as to her guilt, Mary's dying father still tried to shield his daughter from the consequences of her blindly following her heart and Cranstoun's machinations. Mary turned and left the room. Father and daughter parted for the last time.

Dr Addington had by now carried out some scientific tests, albeit elementary, on the unidentified powder in the paper packet and the residue from the gruel pot passed to him for examination by Norton. When he called again on Monday, on finding his patient much worse, as Addington 'apprehended Mr. Blandy to be in the utmost danger, and that this affair might come before a Court of judicature' he decided to send for his colleague, Dr William Lewis, of Oxford, thinking it prudent to seek an additional medical opinion from a physician like-minded in the burgeoning field of chemical analysis. Lewis was a chemist as well as a physician, known for his writings related to pharmacy and medicine, and for his research into metals. The first of his chief academic works of note, *A Course of Practical Chemistry*, had been published in 1746.

When Addington asked Francis Blandy whether or not he himself had 'taken poison often', surprisingly he responded in the affirmative, however on further enquiry, with tears in his eyes, he said that it had been given him by 'A poor love-sick girl' in reference to Mary. When Dr Lewis arrived from Oxford, he confirmed his colleague's diagnosis of poisoning, and on both their instructions, that evening Mary was confined to her room. Although she 'begged to have the liberty to listen at the door where he [her father] died' Mary 'was not allowed it'. To secure her house-arrest a guard was posted at her door, and her keys, papers and 'all instruments wherewith she could hurt either herself or any other person', which included her garters and shoe buckles, were removed, in case she should attempt to commit suicide. One wonders, in the circumstances, whether taking her own life had occurred to Mary as an exit option. Yet when she spoke at her trial it was clear she was affronted by the inference, as in her words she regarded suicide as the last resort of the 'most abandoned creature'.

During her confinement, Addington took it upon himself to question Mary. Did she really pretended to believe that the powders were a harmless 'love philtre'? Why, if the powders were innocuous, did Cranstoun go to the trouble of disguising their description as 'powder to clean the pebbles with'? And in view of her father's grave condition, had she not thought it expedient to summon a physician sooner? Furthermore, why had she concealed what she knew to be the true cause of her father's illness? All pertinent questions, which the prosecution would make much of later, and to which Mary was unable to give any satisfactory reply, other than to protest that from the first she had been deceived by Cranstoun. Maintaining that she had never put powder in anything her father swallowed, with the exception of the gruel drunk by him on the preceding Monday and Tuesday evenings, and only then in the belief that it 'would make him kind to him [Cranstoun] and her,' Mary added that she did not know the powder to be poison 'till she had seen its effects', 'that villain' having assured her that they were nothing other than 'of a very innocent nature'. Mary did, however, make one highly damaging admission during this interview; that about six weeks before, she had put some of the powder into her father's tea, the same cup from which Susannah Gunnell had drunk, she being taken ill for a week afterwards. To all who held her to be a faithless daughter, through her own admission Mary had shown that long before she had introduced the powder into her father's gruel, circumstances must have alerted her to the potentially harmful effects of her actions.

By the following Tuesday, 13 August, Francis Blandy had deteriorated to a delirious and 'excessively weak' state. Though his condition worsened throughout the day, the next morning he seemed to rally, and regaining consciousness for an hour or so, spoke of making his will in a day or two's time, but the remission was brief. He soon relapsed, and fading fast, Addington and Lewis went to Mary's room to tell her that nothing could be done to save her father's life now. Francis Blandy drew his last breath around two o'clock on the afternoon of Wednesday, 14 August 1751.

Chapter 7

'My honour to him will prove my ruin ...'

With her father now dead, Mary declared herself 'one of the most wretched orphans that ever lived'. In spite of their reasonable suspicions, that afternoon Mary's uncles the Reverend Stevens and Charles Blandy condoned with her, and according to Mary's *Own Account* 'occasioned such a moving scene, as is impossible for any human pen to describe'. Pacing the house like 'a frantic distracted person', others who had occasion to observe her behaviour at this time were to testify that Mary's extreme agitation arose from anxiety regarding her own situation, however, and that she showed no sign of sorrow, compassion, or even remorse over her father's death. Of course, it may well have been that Mary was in the reactionary phase of shock; her father had just died after all, and with the barely cold corpse of Francis Blandy laying under the same roof, awaiting post-mortem investigation, the findings of which would be presented at an inquest due to be held the next day. As a consequence, she found herself in a certainly damning situation. Mary was later to assert 'that no stress ought to be laid on any part of my conduct at this time'. Indeed, her acute mental crisis may have coloured her initial behaviour, though clearly Dr Addington thought otherwise; when the defence counsel invited the doctor to say that Mary's anxiety 'proceeded solely from concern for her father', although Addington initially excused himself from expressing any opinion, on being pressed to do so, he said that her agitation 'struck him as due entirely to fears for herself'; he perceived no impressions of grief for her father.

Though Addington's observations may have been harsh, his opinion was reinforced by Mary's next actions. Though she was held under close confinement in her chamber, the household servants nevertheless had access to her room, and later in the afternoon, Mary asked the footman, Robert Harman, whether he would assist in her escape (to France according to one account). Offering him the sizeable inducement of five hundred pounds if he would do so, Harman may well have been dubious about Mary being in possession of such a large sum of money, and keen not to implicate himself. He refused. That night, at Mary's request, the Blandys' cook, Betty, sat up with her and was to receive a similar offer, though the amount of the bribe in this instance was considerably reduced. As soon as they were alone in her room Mary asked 'Betty, will you go away with me? If you will go to the Lion or the Bell and hire a post-chaise, I will give you fifteen guineas when you get into it, and ten guineas more when we come to London.' The significant reduction in the amount offered as a bribe to Betty may well have stemmed from Mary's realistic reassessment of the ready cash available to her. Whether the cook shared the same apprehensions as the footman, Robert Harman, she also declined the offer. At this refusal, Mary burst into laughter and said, 'I was only in a joke, did you think I was in earnest?' Her protestations of jest aside, Mary was later dismissive that either of these conversations had taken place.

In spite of her denial, it would seem that Mary was nevertheless intent on escape, the possibility of which was rendered all the more feasible in view of the person charged with watching over her house arrest. Edward Herne, the sexton of Henley's parish church, who some twelve years prior had been in Mr Blandy's employ, was the person who had been set to guard her door. Herne, however, was to prove a more than accommodating warder. In the past Herne had been amongst those local gentlemen who had sought Mary's hand in marriage. Needless to say, with regard to his lowly station in life, his offer had been pointedly refused by Francis Blandy. But it may have been that Herne was still more than a little in love with Mary. Certainly, he was willing to assist her. At ten o'clock on the morning of Thursday 15 August, Herne, fulfilling his role as sexton, conveniently absented himself in order to dig Francis's grave. While he was thus occupied, unguarded Mary slipped out of her room and ran out of the house. However, in her hasty bid for freedom, as she had had little time to dress herself (in the circumstances she could hardly have summoned one of the household maids to dress her) with 'nothing on but a half-sack and petticoat without a hoop' Mary's dishevelled appearance, not to mention her agitated state attracted instant notice as she made her way along Hart Street in the direction of Henley Bridge. Initially, it was the cries of 'Murderess!' from a small group of children that alerted others. In no time the fugitive was surrounded by an angry, baying crowd; the defamatory gossip concerning the circumstances of her father's death having spread quickly, despite the fact that the Coroner's jury was still to sit that day and return a verdict on Francis's suspicious demise. Understandably, the hostility of the townsfolk frightened Mary and breaking away from the mob she made her way over Henley Bridge to the Little Angel Inn, on the Remenham side of the river, there to seek refuge.

Fortunate for her that the obliging landlady, Mrs Davis, closed the inn door against the enraged populace.

There were two other patrons who happened to be at the inn at the time, a Mr Lane and his wife, who must surely have been surprised and unsettled by the furore going on outside, not to mention Mary's disordered and shaken appearance. After calling for 'a pint of wine', presumably to settle her nerves, Mary addressed Mr Lane, and asked 'Sir, you look like a gentleman; what do you think they will do to me?' Lane, who was obviously acquainted with her circumstances, told her that 'she would be committed to the county gaol for trial at the Assizes, when, if her innocence appeared, she would be acquitted; if not, she would suffer accordingly'. Lane's recollection of Mary's impassioned response to this statement would later prove a matter of contention at her trial; stamping her foot on the ground, Mary exclaimed, 'Oh, that damned villain! But why should I blame him? I am more to blame than he, for I gave it him [her father] and *knew* the consequence.' When Mr Lane later appeared in court, on cross-examination, he was unable to swear whether the word Mary used was 'knew' or 'know'. Though a grammatical splitting of hairs, the distinction between past and present tense was nonetheless pivotal, and potentially incriminating. That Mary already 'knew' what the consequences would be could be construed as an admission of her guilt, as opposed to her coming to 'know' the consequences after the fact, arising from her father's death, the inference here being that she had unwittingly dosed her parent with poison. Unfortunately for Mary, in court, the former assertion was to hold sway.

Outside, the threatening shouts and cries on the street were hard to ignore, and attracting the attention of those in authority it was thought best, for Mary's own safety, as well as the fact that she presented a flight risk, that she be returned to the security of her former house-arrest. Richard Fisher, an alderman of Henley's town council, was sent to retrieve her. A friend of Francis Blandy's, he was also one of the members of the jury selected and summoned to the inquest due to be held later that day. Once he had managed to make his way through the provoked townsfolk surrounding the Little Angel Inn, Fisher was successful in persuading Mary that the best course of action would be for her to return home; but this was easier said than done. Though the distance from the inn to the Blandy house in Hart Street was little over 350 yards, the mood of the crowd was black, and Fisher, along with Robert Stoke who had now been ordered by the mayor to take care of the prisoner, was obliged to bundle Mary in a 'close' post-chaise, that is an enclosed carriage, 'to preserve her from the resentment of the populace'.

Mary was later to refute that she had had any real intention of attempting to escape, and it must be said that the reasons she cited in the following statement held water; that she was in a state of shock after Dr Lewis had advised her that the autopsy on her father's body was to take place that morning:

'Soon after Dr. Lewis came into my room, and I found by him that my poor father's body was to be opened as that morning. As soon as he was gone, I could not bear to stay in the house but walked out. Let reason judge whether I intended an escape. My dress was an half-sack and petticoat, made for a hoop, and the sides very long; neither man nor horse to assist me; and, as they say, I walked as slow as foot could fall; half the town at my heels; and but for the mercy of a woman, who sheltered me in her house, had perhaps lost my life. When I was sent for back by the Justices, the gentlemen who conveyed me to my house, witnessed that I thanked him. Surely this cannot be interpreted an attempt to escape.'

It may have been that Mary was apprehensive of the incriminating evidence that her father's imminent autopsy would reveal, yet in her defence, as it was not unusual for an autopsy to be performed at this time in the deceased's home – a firm kitchen table and adequate lighting were recommended for the purpose – Mary's assertion that she 'could not bear to stay in the house' is also an understandable one.

In view of Edward Herne's dereliction in his duty, this time the Corporation of Henley (the local governing body) sent the serjeant and mace-bearer to take Mary in charge. She must have felt the full gravity of her situation now, as when she asked Richard Fisher how it would go with her, he told her in no uncertain terms, 'very hard' unless she was able to support her story by producing Cranstoun's letters, to which she replied, 'Dear Mr. Fisher, I am afraid I have burnt some that would have brought him to justice. My honour to him will prove my ruin.'

That 'ruin' was brought closer by the findings at Francis Blandy's autopsy. The post-mortem examination performed by Dr Addington and Mr Nicholson, who was the surgeon in Henley, showed that the body was in a generally livid and shrivelled state and that the eyes had bled. The internal organs were found to be discoloured, darker than normal, and stained with bruise-like spots, added to which the inner surface of the stomach and intestines were 'prodigiously inflamed and excoriated' (damaged or eaten away by ulceration). Further, graphic observations followed: these included the muscles of the 'belly' found to be 'very pale and flaccid'; the heart variegated with 'purple spots'; and that the 'lungs resembled bladders half filled with air and blotted in some places with pale, but in most with black ink'. Francis Blandy's liver and spleen were also much discoloured, it being noted that 'the former looked as if it had been boiled'. In short, Addington had 'never found or beheld a body in which the viscera were so universally inflamed and mortified'. Another pertinent, though incorrect finding persuasive to a verdict of death by poisoning was the lack of any apparent natural decay. Such an appearance after death was habitually attributed, by laymen and doctors alike, to the supposed preservative effects of arsenic, when invariably it was the consequence of dehydration, the result of repeated purgings symptomatic to arsenic poisoning, suffered before death. Nevertheless, with the 'opening' and examination of the body complete, Mr Nicholson concurred with Dr Addington's opinion; the findings were indicative of one whose death had been brought about by arsenic poisoning.

Following the autopsy, the inquest into Francis's death was held at the house of Mr John Gale in the town, presided over by Richard Miles, who was the Mayor and the Coroner of Henley. Inquests at this time were often conducted in private homes, even public houses or other public buildings, sometimes with the body present, to be viewed by the jury. The thirteen male jurors – women were not allowed to serve on any jury until the 1919 Sex Disqualification (Removal) Act was passed – were sworn in and:

'charged to enquire for our Sovereign Lord the King, when, where, and by what means and after what fashion the said Francis Blandy came by his death upon their oaths say, that the said Francis Blandy was poisoned; and that they have a strong suspicion, from the depositions of the witnesses, that Mary Blandy, daughter of the said Francis Blandy, did poison and murder her said father Francis Blandy, against the peace of our said Lord the King, his Crown and Dignity.'

Of the witnesses examined, representative of the medical fraternity were Drs Addington and Lewis, Mr Nicholson, the surgeon who had assisted Addington with the autopsy, and the apothecary, Norton. Addington, Lewis and Norton each in turn testified as to the symptoms exhibited by the deceased during life, added to which was the testimony of Addington and Nicholson of the appearance presented by Francis Blandy's body after death. Dr Addington was also questioned with regard to the results of the analysis that he had carried out on the powder found in the gruel pot and that contained in the paper packet retrieved from the kitchen grate. As well as his own tests, Addington had given a sample of the powder to Mr King, an experienced chemist in Reading, for a second opinion. On the basis of the chemical analysis, and the autopsy findings, the doctors, the surgeon and the apothecary were all of the opinion that Francis's cause of death was poison, and that the powder tested was a poison capable of causing death.

Depositions were also taken from the Blandy household servants, from the maid Susannah, Betty the cook and Harman the footman. Mary's old flame, Edward Herne, was also examined. It came as no surprise when, the evidence having been heard, the jury found that Francis Blandy had been poisoned and that his daughter 'did poison and murder her said father'.

The following day, Friday, 16 August, Richard Miles issued the necessary warrant for the constables to convey the prisoner to the county gaol at Oxford, where Mary would be detained until 'discharged by due course of law'.

That night Francis Blandy was buried, next to the grave of his wife, in the chancel of Henley's parish church, St Mary the Virgin. Not one of his relations was present at his funeral, the only mourners being Norton the apothecary, his clerk Robert Littleton and Harman, the footman. The entry made in the burial register dated the following day, 17 August 1751, reads; 'Blandy, Francis', however, an addendum to that entry, presumably made at some later date as it appears in a different hand and ink reads; 'Attorney at Law was poisoned by his only child Mary Blandy'.

In order to avoid any repetition of the public outcry occasioned by Mary's last ill-advised sojourn onto the streets of Henley, when the time came for her to be taken to prison the custodial party set out 'very privately' for Oxford Gaol at four o'clock in the morning following her father's burial, travelling in a Landau, a four-wheeled, convertible carriage. Though the warrant for her committal had been issued on the previous day, Mary had been granted the short delay in order that she could make the arrangements 'necessary for a lengthy visit' to Oxford Gaol. Amongst her personal items, Mary was careful to include her tea chest, its canisters 'all most full of fine Hyson, which she said would save her some Money'. One of the contemporary, and defamatory pamphlets making the rounds after Mary's indictment shows her enjoying a cup of tea in gaol. Attended by two constables, Mary was also accompanied by Mrs Dean, a former servant of the family, whom Mary had requested as her maid. Leaving at such an early hour, escaping universal scorn and scrutiny, the closed carriage reached Oxford, a journey of about twenty-five miles, by eleven o'clock that morning.

When she arrived, Oxford Gaol must certainly have appeared foreboding to Mary as it was housed in what was formerly Oxford Castle. Like many town castles around England, after the Civil War it was converted for use as a prison, a purpose it served until 1996, later redeveloped as a quirky 'prison themed' modern boutique hotel. As with other prisons at the time, the owners, in this case Oxford's Christ Church College, leased the castle to wardens who would profit by charging prisoners for their board and lodging. All well and good for those who could pay their way; such detainees described as *milch-kine* (milk cows), an old slang term used by gaolers for 'when their prisoners will bleed freely [i.e. part with their money easily] to have some Favour'. Yet prisoners without means were destined to a far more spartan confinement, reliant on the Keeper's daily allocation of bread and beer, for which he received a stipend, a financial arrangement that was open to abuse, and inmates often went without. Massed together in damp, unsanitary conditions which bred 'gaol fever', in such overcrowded conditions, it was not unheard of for some prisoners so tightly packed in the same cell to suffocate to death. There was no privacy, segregation or protection from other prisoners, with all kinds of detainees held together regardless of gender, and including minors, serious criminals and petty criminals alike, sharing their confinement with those awaiting trial and prisoners actually serving a gaol term. Despondency and the prevalent threat of violence and disease, not to the mention the meagre daily rations must have made incarceration in an eighteenth-century gaol akin to hell on earth.

While Oxford had in the past gained a fearsome reputation as a brutal place of incarceration, as a prisoner with means, this was not to be Mary's experience, however. Her first question on arriving at the gaol was, 'Am I to be fettered?' and, on learning that she would not be put into leg irons, so long as she behaved well, she remarked, 'I have wore them all this morning in my mind in the coach.' Despite her worst imaginings, during the weeks leading up to Mary's trial, 'her imprisonment was indeed rather like a retirement from the world than the confinement of a criminal'. With her maid to attend her and the best rooms in the Keeper's house at her disposal, Mary took tea twice daily, from her personal supply of Hyson, and was allowed morning and afternoon to take a turn in the Keeper's garden, while the evenings were spent playing cards.

The matter of Mary's privacy was also strictly respected; no one was permitted access to the prisoner without permission, and with regards to visitors, none was allowed to see her 'without her consent'. As many keepers or warders were known to exploit their position, profiting from charging a fee for showing visitors around the cells, especially those of 'celebrity' inmates, the scruples of the Keeper of Oxford Gaol nevertheless did him credit, he declining the 'very extraordinary sums' apparently offered as a bribe on a daily basis from those keen to set eyes on his prisoner. Mary's partial liberty and her pleasant walks in the garden were soon to be curtailed, however, when a rumour reached the authorities in London that a plan was afoot to break Mary out of gaol – her fears of being 'fettered' were at length to be realised.

Whether it was the physical discomfort, or the indignity of being shackled that was Mary's primary concern, on 25 October, the Secretary of State intervened and instructed the Sheriff of the county 'to take more particular care of her', upon which order the fetters were well and truly riveted on. In a contemporary image entitled *Miss Molly Blandy, taken from the life in Oxford Castle*, Mary is depicted in the highly fashionable attire of the day, but with the less than modish accessory of leg irons encircling her ankles above her dainty shoes. Indeed, the restraints were to prove a physical discomfort as one of Mary's visitors was to comment that her leg was:

'considerably swelled, and the Red Cloth wch [sic] was round the Iron before has been cut off to give her room, but it is still so close, as renders it impossible to be slipt over her Heel.'

On top of the ignominy of the fetters, a further blow was to be communicated from the outside world. Mary learnt from a visitor, clearly one from the approved list, the astonishing news that her father's fortune, to which Mary was the sole heiress, in fact amounted to less than £4,000, clearly falling far short of the £10,000 so widely boasted of. The agonising irony was, of course, that the exaggerated sum had been the entire raison d'être for Cranstoun's engineering her father's death, and Mary's ultimate ruination. In contemplation of all that had gone before, Mary's demeanour altered; she stepped up the frequency of former scant attendances to divine service in the prison chapel, and prayer replaced the pleasantries of taking tea and playing cards. And now the prison chaplain, the Reverend John Swinton, was her only visitor.

With regards to setting a date for Mary's trial, ordinarily there would have been no problem with this being held over until the next Lent Assizes. Depending on the severity of an accusation, prisoners could spend some considerable time on remand awaiting trial before the Assize Courts, or 'Great Sessions', normally held twice a year during Lent and summer. However, there were serious concerns over the delay in Mary's case coming to trial in view of the precarious health of two of the material witnesses. It was feared that the elderly Susannah Gunnell and the old charlady Ann Emmet 'could not long survive the effects of the poison they partook of' and that either one of them, or both, might 'dye' before the Lent proceedings of the following year.

The Lord Chancellor, Philip Yorke, 1st Earl Hardwicke, had written on 27 September 1751 to the Duke of Newcastle, the Secretary of State, advising that 'if upon the examinations there appeared to be sufficient grounds to proceed against Mary Blandy for her father's murder,' that the expense of the prosecution should be met by the Crown. This meant that the trial date could be expedited and Mary's case heard 'at the King's Bench Bar within the next Term' – an unusual but not unprecedented practice. Ordinarily, the eighteenth-century legal system relied primarily on victims and other private individuals to initiate and bear the cost of prosecutions, but in this instance, the Lord Chancellor was keen to move matters along, concerned that it would be a 'Reproach to the King's justice should so flagrant a crime escape punishment' as might happen if the prosecution were left in private hands, and the court denied the testimonies of the two seemingly ailing witnesses.

Accordingly, Mr Sharpe, the Solicitor to the Treasury, was ordered to take the necessary steps, under direction of the Attorney-General; it would, however, be procedurally necessary for a special commission to be sent to Berkshire, to find a Bill of Indictment there, before the trial could be heard at the Court of King's Bench in London, rather than at the Oxford Assizes.

In theory, this was an expedient decision, in view of the shaky constitutions of Susannah and Ann, however, matters were to be considerably delayed by the wrangling and blame-laying arising from the botched attempts in apprehending Cranstoun. Shortly after Mary's committal, Richard Lowe, the Mayor of Henley's messenger, had been despatched to Scotland with a view to arresting Cranstoun as an accessory to Francis Blandy's murder. From the address on Mary's letter, intercepted by Robert Littleton, Cranstoun was believed to be in Berwickshire. However, when an application for the necessary warrant was made to Mr Carre, the Sheriff-Depute of that county, he apparently 'made some difficulty' over the request, and by the time it was eventually granted, Cranstoun was long gone. Lowe and Carre each blamed the other for the failure to arrest the now fugitive Cranstoun, the delay then further exacerbated by the Lord Chancellor weighing in, recommending that the Lord Justice-Clerk of Scotland be requested to hold an inquiry into the facts himself. While Carre was to be completely exonerated from the charges of negligence made against him by Lowe, the upshot of this administrative hiatus meant that Mary's case would now not be brought to trial until the Lent Assizes of 1752.

Ideally, as the Lord Chancellor was to point out in private correspondence with the Duke of Newcastle, a warrant issued by the Secretary of State, 'which runs equally over the whole kingdom' would have been more judicious. As matters stood, with the debacle in securing the warrant at the Scottish end, 'so many persons must be apprised of it, that he [Cranstoun] could hardly fail of getting notice'. The conjecture that Cranstoun had by now 'gone beyond sea' indeed proved founded. The captain was now in France.

With the discreet financial assistance of his family, the necessary arrangements enabling Cranstoun's flight had hastily been made. Through the agency of a network of family friends, namely that of Lord Home, the services of one Francis Gropptty, who had 'lived with Lord Home several years' and at that time 'did business for him' were secured to get Cranstoun as far as Calais. As no order to stop Cranstoun at Dover had yet been issued, presumably Gropptty was confident that he ran no personal risk to himself in assisting with the escape. However, when on 2 September, as arranged, Cranstoun appeared at Gropptty's house in Mount Street, he explained that he was without funds for the journey, having been 'rob'd' of his money and portmanteau on his way to London. Gropptty took Cranstoun's claims at face value, and presuming that he would later receive appropriate recompense, purchased for the traveller 'such, necessaries as he wanted'. Gropptty was also to advance ten guineas of his own money when the loan of twenty pounds, which Cranstoun had apparently solicited from another family friend, was not forthcoming.

Cranstoun and Gropptty set out that same day in a post-chaise for Dover, where they arrived at nine o'clock the next morning. On 4 September they embarked on a 'packet ship' bound for Calais. 'Packets' were vessels which offered a regularly scheduled service, carrying post office mail, and packets, as the name suggests, as well as paying passengers. The cost of their passage was a guinea, though if rough weather were to prevent safe entry into the French harbour, the shrewd local boatmen would have charged more than they had paid to cross the Channel to row them ashore with their luggage; in that eventuality, Cranstoun would doubtless have defrayed the outlay from the money he had already conned out of his obliging travelling companion.

Once Gropptty had safely installed his charge in lodgings at 'the Rate of Fifty Livres a Month', he left Calais and returned to London.

Though he was promised 'a handsome reward for his trouble' Gropptty said that as he had acted solely out of gratitude to Lord Home, he wanted nothing more than his expenses, which, including the ten guineas advanced to Cranstoun, amounted to eighteen pounds. When Gropptty signed his sworn deposition made on 3 February 1752, however, he was still waiting to be paid.

Chapter 8

Proof of the Perfect Poison

While Cranstoun was enjoying his liberty on French soil, his fettered fiancée was preparing herself for trial. In the preparation of her defence, Mary's first choice of attorney was Mr Newell, a Henley man who had succeeded her father as town clerk. After the initial consultation, however, Mr Newell's services were dispensed with when he tactlessly expressed his astonishment that Mary should have landed herself in her current situation over such 'a mean-looking little ugly fellow' as Cranstoun. Affronted, Mary employed the services of Mr Rivers, an attorney from Woodstock, instead.

Rivers had his work cut out. From the day of Mary's arrest, all sorts of rumours had begun to circulate; that as well as poisoning her father, Mary had also poisoned her mother; that she had even poisoned her mother's friend, Mrs Pocock. The circumstances of this lady's death are not known, other than that the executors of her will later sold the manor at Turville to a John Osborne in 1753; Mary was, however, to reference her innocence in respect of both these spurious allegations in her last address from the gallows. Furthermore, Mary was supposedly still corresponding with Cranstoun, and there was even the scandalous suggestion that while she was imprisoned awaiting trial, that she had secretly married the Keeper's son, 'to which the circumstances of their acquaintance left her no alternative' – the inference here is clear. The gossip-mill continued to grind loudly. It was said that Mary's fortune - though diminished, the sum still represented a hefty inheritance – was being employed to bribe the authorities and to pay for the convenient 'removal' of principal witnesses, while she herself had made repeated attempts to escape. With regards to the desultory attacks made on her character, Mary herself was to complain that:

'It has been said that I am a wretched drunkard, a prophane [sic] swearer, that I never went to chapel, contemned all holy ordinances, and in short gave myself up to all kinds of immorality.'

Even before Mary appeared at the bar, the pamphlets and publications damning her name poured from the presses. Eagerly devoured by a public hungry for the gossip and rumour surrounding such high-profile cases, the scurrilous popularity and circulation of such disclosures were great at the time. An increasingly competitive business, with the advent of cheap printing from the seventeenth century on, publishers profited by touting the often embellished and lurid details of the supposed histories and scandalous crimes of 'celebrity criminals'. Cases such as Mary's were also prominently featured in the contemporary newspapers of the day; with significant column space given over to accounts presenting the 'true facts', it had become increasingly clear to newspaper proprietors, not only that crime sold but in particular the taste for exaggerated reports of murder was pervasive. Outweighing the ideals of morality and the reassurance that justice had been served, then as now feeding the appetite for sensationalised copy proved profitable.

While the delay in bringing Mary's case to trial afforded the speculative press more time in which to capitalise on her impending judgement, finally, on Monday, 2 March 1752, the grand jury for the county of Oxford found a true bill of indictment against Mary Blandy. The long-anticipated trial was about to begin. However, as the Town Hall, where the Assizes were usually held, was 'then rebuilding' (the refurbishments would not be completed until July of that year) and as the University authorities refused use of the Sheldonian Theatre, the official ceremonial hall of the University of Oxford, the hall of the Divinity School was instead selected to be the venue for Mary's trial the following day. In Oxford, justice was administered by two separate legal systems; one for Gown and one for Town, 'Gown' being the university community, 'Town' being the non-academic population. This arrangement made for strained relations, rooted in elitism on the one hand and resentment on the other, the apparent leniency in 'Gown' sentencing held to be a highbrow and unfair judicial distinction. As matters stood, the University were gracious enough to allow the use of the hall where the Vice-Chancellor's Court was ordinarily held.

The proceedings of Tuesday 3 March were to get off to a late start, however, as owing to some nocturnal shenanigans, presumably mischievously meant and intended as a ploy to delay the day, it was found that 'a small stone or other obstruction' had been jammed into the keyhole of the Hall door, necessitating the lock to be broken open. After the exertion of some brute force, once access was gained the judges, who had repaired to their lodgings while the situation was remedied, duly returned at eight o'clock, and Mary Blandy was placed at the bar to answer the charges laid against her.

Presiding over the case were the Honourable Heneage Legge and Sir Sidney Stafford Smythe, both Barons of His Majesty's Court of Exchequer. Appearing for the Crown were the Honourable Mr Bathurst and Mr Serjeant Hayward, and assisting in the prosecution were the Honourable Mr Barrington and Messrs Hayes, Nares, and Ambler. Mary's defence was to be conducted by Mr Ford, assisted by Messrs Morton and Aston. While Bathurst was destined to rise to the office of Lord Chancellor, of Mary's defence counsel only Richard Aston rose to any eminence; appointed King's Counsel in 1759, in 1761 Aston was made lord chief justice of the Court of Common Pleas in Ireland. However, few English judges proved themselves a popular choice in Ireland, and Aston, noted for his brusque manner, was not of their number. In 1765 he resigned his Irish post and was transferred to the English court, sitting as a judge on the King's Bench, and knighted accordingly.

On that Tuesday morning, the long chamber of the Divinity Hall was packed to capacity, the eager crowds who had surged through the doorway at one point jostling Mary on her way to the bar. Some determined onlookers even resorted to forcing their way in through open windows in order to get a glimpse of the accused, occasioning Bathurst in his initial address to observe that he was not surprised 'at this vast concourse of people collected together,' in view of the 'heinous nature of the crime'.

In the March edition of *The London Magazine* for 1752, England's oldest literary periodical, in the account of Mary's trial, the editor was careful to include a note of her dress and appearance when she appeared in court. Described as '… of a middle stature, rather plump than slender, of no delicate shape' the article went on to note that Mary '… had a large straight nose, full mouth, flattish cheeks; dark hair and eye brows, fine sprightly black eyes, and appeared, as she really was, to be about 35 years of age'. Mary was in fact 31 years old at the time. Mention was also made of Mary's attire, that her 'dress was chosen with great propriety;' plain and neat, of black bombazine, a fine twilled fabric usually of silk and worsted or cotton, traditionally dyed black for mourning wear, and her headdress comprising of a white linen kerchief, 'covered with a crape shade and hood'. Perhaps Mary was following the old advice; wear to court what you would wear to church. A chair had been provided for her, in case she felt fatigued – she was still fettered in leg irons for her court appearance – and her maid, allowed to attend to her in the courtroom, was also by her side. As the indictment was read aloud, many people noticed that she remained 'sedate and composed'; in fact, she was to remain self-possessed and dry-eyed throughout the entire proceedings, which lasted for thirteen hours, saving for one tear, involuntarily shed when Mrs Mounteney, her mother's friend and Mary's godmother, later gave evidence against her. On leaving the witness-box, Mrs Mounteney seized Mary's hand, saying 'God bless you!' prompting Mary's only momentary lapse in composure, but after drinking a glass of wine and water, she 'resumed her air of stoical indifference'.

Charged with 'not having the fear of God before your eyes, but being moved and seduced by the instigation of the devil, and of your malice aforethought, contriving and intending, him the said Francis Blandy, your said late father, in his lifetime, to deprive of his life, and him feloniously to kill and murder', to this arraignment Mary entered a plea of 'not guilty'.

The jury having been duly sworn in, Mr Bathurst began his address for the Crown, followed by Hayward, who, in spite of his rather more rhetorical and florid style, added little to the facts of which the jury was already aware. Hayward could not, however, resist including in his address an admonition to the numerous 'young gentlemen of this University' who were present, of 'the dreadful consequences of disobedience to a parent'. The Crown's case then opened with the medical witnesses, Drs Addington and Lewis, and Mr Norton the apothecary.

In his *Science and the Criminal*, published in 1911, the chemist and forensic scientist Ainsworth Mitchell made note of the fact that Mary Blandy's case was 'remarkable as being the first one of which there is any detailed record, in which convincing scientific proof of poisoning was given'. Indeed, this was the first time that detailed medical evidence had been presented in court on a charge of murder by poisoning, and consequently the first time a conviction was secured on the basis of such evidence. As previously mentioned, the considerable public attention garnered by Addington's appearing as the principal and expert for the prosecution was to make the doctor's career, yet his appearance, and testimony, were also pivotal in paving the way for the advancement in, and later acceptance of scientific testing in a court of law.

Although Addington had not been able to chemically analyse Francis Blandy's organs for traces of arsenic, as the technology for such an analysis did not exist at the time, the doctor was nevertheless able to convince the court, on the basis of observed comparisons, that the powder Mary had put in her father's tea and gruel was indeed arsenic. Though Addington's methods were rudimentary by today's standards of forensic examination, his evaluations would go on to lay the groundwork for successive chemists, most notably James Marsh, who would later formulate a conclusive test of his own. Publishing his findings in *The Edinburgh Philosophical Journal* in 1836,

Marsh had devised the first reliable analysis that showed scientifically that arsenic was present in the body of a victim, his efforts having been spurred on by the outcome of a failed murder trial in 1832, where he had appeared as an expert witness for the prosecution. The case was that of John Bodle, accused of poisoning his grandfather with arsenic-laced coffee. Marsh had performed the standard test at the time, mixing a suspected sample with hydrogen sulphide and hydrochloric acid, and while he was able to detect the presence of arsenic as yellow arsenic trisulphide, when he came to show his findings to the jury the sample had deteriorated. Even if it had remained stable, however, there was still the distinct possibility that Bodle would have walked free as juries were often loath to convict on forensic evidence alone. An artful defence lawyer could also play on a jury's lack of scientific knowledge regarding chemical analysis, the confusion leading them to disregard it and return a verdict of not guilty. Nevertheless, it was Bodle's acquittal on the grounds of 'reasonable doubt' that was to prove the impetus for Marsh to go to develop an irrefutable method of evidential detection – the 'Marsh Test' as it commonly became known. The mere existence of this test alone was to prove a deterrent; the sharp decline in the number of cases of deliberate arsenic poisoning exemplifying that arsenic had lost its appeal as the 'perfect' murder weapon. A distinction that was hard to shake, long since regarded as the 'perfect poison', arsenic was ideal because it was colourless and tasteless and could be disguised in a cup of strong tea or coffee, or a glass of brandy, or incorporated in the preparation of semi-solid foods. Furthermore, the symptoms exhibited by the victim were similar to those stricken with cholera, and death by arsenic poisoning was often misattributed to the disease rather than to murderous intent.

Prior to the development of the Marsh Test, at the time of Mary's trial the field of forensic toxicology was still in its relative infancy. Though Addington's evidential presentation appeared elementary, it was nevertheless ground-breaking, and certainly an improvement on some of the former and rather more basic practices of detecting the presence of poison in a victim's body. Prior to 1788 there were no comprehensive guidelines on how autopsies should be performed. Some doctors and surgeons had little idea of what to look for, besides which the examination techniques they employed also varied. The findings revealed by a standard, and it must be said, unsophisticated post mortem were regarded as questionable by many jurors. In lieu of any concrete medical opinion then, or acceptance of the same, reliance was placed on the most basic of circumstantial evidence, and it was thought that comparable observations of the effects on animals, either accidentally ingesting or being deliberately fed samples of supposedly poisonous substances, was a reliable indicator of foul play. Even into the next century, initial suspicions excited by such coincidental comparisons were to provide the impetus for an accusation; in 1835, Yorkshire housewife Ursula Lofthouse was hanged, having been found guilty of poisoning her husband with two pennyworths of arsenic, purchased from her local apothecary. Though it was initially assumed that her husband had contracted cholera, the presumption of poisoning was reinforced by the swift demise of four of the chickens which Ursula kept, the birds having died after pecking at some of Robert Lofthouse's vomit. Likewise, the rumours which had begun to spread about the Edinburgh poisoner William Bennison, who murdered his wife in 1850, were initially aroused when two of his neighbour's dogs died after both had scavenged the cooked potatoes put out by Bennison on the night of his wife's death.

Addington's efforts then were a step-up in an era when rigorous autopsies were infrequent, and chemical tests virtually unheard of. Even if medical opinion were available, it was not routinely sought. The difficulty in determining whether a deliberate act of criminality had taken place often meant that it was equally likely that an innocent person would be convicted and hanged as it would be for a guilty party to walk free. And though the results of Addington's tests would not hold up in a court of law today, they were nevertheless at the forefront of forensic advancement, as highlighted during the doctor's cross-examination at Mary's trial when his methods were explained to the court.

When questioned as to whether he had conducted experiments on both the powder retrieved from the gruel pot, so assiduously delivered into Mrs Mounteney's care by the maid Susannah Gunnell, and the powder contained in the unburned packet rescued from the kitchen-grate at Hart Street, Addington stated that he had given 'the greatest part of the first to Mr King, an experienced chemist in Reading, and desired that he would examine it, which he did, and he told me that it was white arsenic'. The remainder of the sample from the gruel pot and the powder from the paper packet were used in trials made by Addington himself.

When he was asked why he believed the powders to be white arsenic, Addington presented the following observations, and in his own words, these were that:

'(1) This powder has a milky whiteness; so has white arsenic. (2) This is gritty and almost insipid; so is white arsenic. (3) Part of it swims on the surface of cold water, like a pale sulphurous film, but the greatest part sinks to the bottom, and remains there undissolved; the same is true of white arsenic. (4) This thrown on red-hot iron does not flame, but rises entirely in thick white fumes, which have the stench of garlic, and cover cold iron held just over them with white flowers; white arsenic does the same. [The 'white flowers' refers to the white arsenic that forms a deposit on the iron when the grey elemental arsenic combines with oxygen and cools.] (5) I boiled 10 grains of this powder in 4 ounces of clean water, and then, passing the decoction through a filter, divided it into five equal parts, which were put into as many glasses—into one glass I poured a few drops of spirit of sal ammoniac, into another some of the lixivium of tartar, into the third some strong spirit of vitriol, into the fourth some spirit of salt, and into the last some syrup of violets. The spirit of sal ammoniac threw down a few particles of pale sediment. The lixivium of tartar gave a white cloud, which hung a little above the middle of the glass. The spirits of vitriol and salt made a considerable precipitation of lightish coloured substance, which, in the former hardened into glittering crystals, sticking to the sides and bottom of the glass. Syrup of violets produced a beautiful pale green tincture. Having washed the sauce pan, funnel, and glasses used in the foregoing experiments very clean, and provided a fresh filter, I boiled 10 grains of white arsenic, bought of Mr. Wilcock, druggist in Reading, in four ounces of clean water, and, filtering and dividing it into five equal parts, proceeded with them just as I had done with the former decoctions. There was an exact similitude between the experiments made on the two decoctions. They corresponded so nicely in each trial that I declare I never saw any two things in Nature more alike the decoction made with the powder found in Mr. Blandy's gruel and that made with white arsenic. From these experiments, and others which I am ready to produce if desired, I believe that powder to be white arsenic.'

Addington added that Mr Wilcock, the druggist who had provided the control sample of arsenic, had 'weighed both the powder and the white arsenic' and was present throughout while he conducted these experiments.

The expert testimony concluded, regardless of whether or not anyone present in the courtroom was aware that these forensic tests were in no way definitive, nor specific to arsenic alone, further damning testimony was to flow from the witness box over the course of the succeeding hours.

The physical appearance of the principal witness for the prosecution, Susannah Gunnell, must have been visually detrimental in itself, even if the evidence that she gave was fair-minded. Susannah was obviously still suffering the effects of her accidental ingestion of the poison intended for Francis Blandy, as she was described as being 'wore down to a Skelliton [sic]'. After the material facts and the circumstances of her ill health had been established, Susannah was asked about Mary's behaviour toward her father. She stated that although Mary would sometimes 'talk very affectionately'; at other times 'she would say he was an old villain for using an only child in such a manner'. Further questioning concerning Mary's relationship with her father revealed that while 'Her general behaviour was dutiful, except upon any passion or a hasty word from her father', that 'Sometimes she wished for him long life, sometimes for his death'. Susannah was to add that in the event of her father's death, Mary had said 'she would go to Scotland and live with Lady Cranstoun'. The final line of questioning sought to clarify whether or not Mary had been aware that the gruel served to her father had been the cause of his illness – Susannah's reply was that 'She knew he was ill, but I cannot tell whether she knew the cause of it'; however, as it was clear that Mary must have been aware that the same gruel had occasioned Ann Emmet's violent purgings, this was construed as further proof of her guilt.

The testimony of Betty Binfield was to prove more damaging, however. She said that when her mistress had spoken to the maids of the death portent that the appearance of Francis's wraith to Cranstoun had foretold, that she was glad of it 'for that then she would soon be released from all her fatigues, and be happy'. Betty said she had also heard Mary cursing her father, calling him 'rascal and villain,' and that on one occasion she had supposedly remarked, 'Who would grudge to send an old father to hell for £10,000?' It would, however, appear that Betty was certainly something of a hostile witness, as highlighted in the defence counsel's cross-examination. When Betty was asked whether she had any 'ill-will' against her mistress, though she maintained that 'I always told her I wished her very well,' when Betty was asked if she had ever said of Mary 'Damn her for a black bitch; I should be glad to see her go up the ladder and be hanged', the cook's cheeks may have reddened a little, but her confident response was, 'No, sir, I never did in my life.'

With regards to the evidence of the old charwoman, Ann Emmet, the concerns over the probable deterioration in her failing health, occasioned by the delay in the case coming to trial were indeed to prove founded. According to the testimony of her daughter Alice, who was called in her stead, Ann was 'now very ill', and in no condition to give evidence in court. Though the prosecution was deprived of the opportunity of presenting this material witness, Addington nevertheless attested to the fact that he had attended professionally on both Susannah and Ann, and that their symptoms, in his opinion, were those of arsenical poisoning. As an 'expert' witness, Addington was permitted to give evidence of both facts and *opinion*, in order to assist the judge and jury to decide upon the verdict.

In view of the testimonies already heard, in addition to those of the subsequent witnesses, the weight of evidence against Mary was seemingly incriminating enough. When Robert Littleton was called, Francis's clerk who had read and revealed the contents of Mary's fateful letter to Cranstoun, though he gave his evidence with 'manifest' regret, he was nevertheless to admit that he frequently heard Mary curse her father in such terms as 'rogue', 'villain', and 'toothless old dog'. The testimony of Robert Harman, the footman to whom Mary had supposedly offered the £500 bribe to assist in her flight, must have blackened her case even further. Following the evidence given by Mr Fisher, who had been instrumental in reinstating Mary's house arrest, and to whom she had expressed her concerns over burning Cranstoun's correspondence, and that of Mr and Mrs Lane, who had been at the Little Angel Inn on the day of her attempted flight, as final evidence, Mary's incriminating letter to Cranstoun, intercepted by Littleton was submitted. The case for the Crown rested.

It was now time for Mary's case to be made. While defence counsels were allowed to call and examine their own witnesses, as well as cross-examine those called by the prosecution, they were not permitted to address the jury directly. It was not until 1836 that defence counsels would have a right to address the jury, after the passing of the Prisoners' Counsel Act in that year. Mary's defence team might also have been hobbled by any evidence put forward by the prosecution of which they had been kept ignorant. Before the witnesses for the defence were called, however, Mary was allowed to make a speech on her own behalf.

Having benefited from a reasonable education, Mary may have written the speech, or some of it, herself, though it may have been prepared for her beforehand by her counsel. Elucidating on the various slights, injustices and misrepresented falsehoods to which Mary felt herself the victim, she declared that, 'My misfortunes have been, and are such, as never woman felt before.' She also alluded to the unfairness of her detractors who before her case had even come to trial had 'published papers and depositions which ought not to have been published in order to represent me as the most abandoned of my sex and to prejudice the world against me'. And while she made little attempt to refute the damning evidence which had been presented in court against her, she nevertheless protested that she was 'as innocent as the child unborn of the death of my father', adding that she 'really thought the powder an innocent, inoffensive thing,' intended to procure her father's love, not bring about his death, adding that 'I would not endeavour to save my life at the expense of truth'. Any defence counsel worth their salt must have shrewdly advised as to the importance of emphasising the matter of Mary's supposed ignorance, as it was the question of Mary's knowing full well the true nature of the powder upon which the verdict, and her life, hung. Mary concluded by saying:

> 'It has been mentioned, I should say I was ruined. My lords, when a young woman loses her character is not that her ruin? Why, then, should this expression be construed in so wide a sense? Is it not ruining my character to have such a thing laid to my charge? And whatever may be the event of this trial I am ruined most effectually.'

Mary's speech concluded, the witnesses selected by her defence counsel were called. The testimony of the first, Ann James, who was a washerwoman on the Blandy domestic staff, would seem to undermine Betty's denial of any hostile and prejudicial feelings she had toward her mistress, reinforcing Mary's objection to 'that witness' being 'inspired with vindictive sentiments'. Ann James related how there had been 'a difference between Elizabeth Binfield and Miss Blandy', the upshot of which was that 'Binfield was to go away'. Whether of her own volition or as a consequence of being dismissed is not clear. Furthermore, after Mary had been removed to Oxford Gaol, Ann related how she had overheard Betty's defamatory references to Mary, as did the next witness called, Mary Banks, though her recollection was that the uncomplimentary words were spoken while Mary was still in the house, on 'the night Mr. Blandy was opened', the autopsy having been performed on Thursday 15 August.

Betty was then recalled, and on cross-examination changed her tune somewhat, and admitted to 'a little quarrel' between herself and her mistress, but maintained that she had 'never said such words' with regards to damning Mary as a 'black bitch' that she would be glad to see hanged.

Edward Herne, that former admirer of Mary's who had conveniently absented himself from guard duty on the day of her brief escape from the Hart Street house, was the next witness called. He gave Mary a high character reference, saying that in the eighteen years of their acquaintance, he being a regular visitor to the house as often as four times a week, and that he had 'never heard her swear an oath all the time I have known her, or speak a disrespectful word of her father'. Furthermore, when cross–examined by the prosecution with regards as to whether Mary had any 'design to hurt her father', Herne stated that Miss Blandy had confided in him that '... when Cranstoun put the powder into the tea, [August 1750] upon which no damage at all came, when she put powder afterwards herself, she apprehended no damage could come to her father'. While he was still on the stand, however, the prosecution took the opportunity to capitalise on a potentially incriminating conversation which had taken place between Herne and Mary on an occasion when he had visited her in gaol. During that, Mary had seemingly inferred her guilt equal to Cranstoun's; when Herne had made Mary aware of a bogus report of Cranstoun's arrest, she had apparently 'wrung her hands' and said, 'I hope in God it is true, that he may be brought to justice as well as I, and that he may suffer the punishment due to his crime, *as I shall do for mine*.' At this point, for the first time in the proceedings, Mary interjected. Asking leave to direct some questions of her own to the last witness, she was nevertheless advised by Judge Legge that 'You had better tell your questions to your counsel, for you may do yourself harm by asking questions'. Accordingly, her line of enquiry directed through Mr Aston, Mary sought to reinforce that 'no damage' had resulted upon Cranstoun's use of the powder back in August 1750, from which fact she supported her belief that their effects were indeed harmless. Further, concerning the apparent reference to her own guilt in her conversation with Herne, the witness's response was that:

> 'She said she should be glad Cranstoun should be taken and brought to justice; she thought it would bring the whole to light, he being the occasion of it all, for she suffered [by being in prison – hence the 'as I shall do for mine' remark] and was innocent, and knew nothing that it was poison no more than I or any one person in the house.'

Of the testimony of the remaining witnesses, Thomas Cawley and Thomas Staverton, who had been friends of Francis Blandy for upwards of twenty years, alluded in the main to Mary's happy relationship with her father. The next called to the witness stand was Mrs Davis, the landlady of the Angel Inn where Mary had sought refuge after the angry mob had pursued her over the Henley bridge. Her testimony, along with that of the last witness called, Robert Stoke, who had detained Mary on orders from the Mayor, both attested to the fact that on Thursday 15 August, Mary did not appear to either of them to be attempting flight.

The evidence for the defence concluded, in a last effort, Mr Ford highlighted to the court that:

> 'very unjustifiable and illegal methods have been used to prejudice the world against Miss Blandy, such as it is to be hoped, no man will have the boldness to repeat—I mean the printing and publishing the examination of witnesses before her trial'.

In view of the 'very scandalous reports… spread concerning her behaviour ever since her imprisonment', Ford sought to reinforce his point by asking that the Reverend Swinton, the prison chaplain, be called to give some account of his client's excellent conduct whilst in gaol, 'that she may at least be delivered of some of the infamy she at present lies under'.

The response of the honourable judges to this request, however, was that it was needless to call a further witness to testify to Mary's character and behaviour, as the jury had been firmly directed to consider only what was deposed in Court, and to entirely disregard the defamatory reports appearing in any scurrilous papers and pamphlets which had been printed before the hearing, or any other reports, printed or hearsay, whatsoever.

It was now Mr Bathurst's turn to rejoinder for the Crown:

> 'Your lordships will, I hope, indulge me in a very few words by way of reply, and after the length of evidence which has been laid before the jury I will take up but little of your lordships' time. It has been proved to a demonstration that Mr. Francis Blandy did die of poison. It is as clearly proved that he died of the poison put into his water gruel upon the 5th of August, and that the prisoner at the bar put it in. For so much appears, not only from her own confession, but from a variety of other evidence. The single question, therefore, for your consideration is, whether she did it knowingly or ignorantly?'

Bathurst was even-handed enough however to endorse the censure of the defence counsel with regard to the circulation of the 'very scandalous reports' spread about Mary, again reminding the jury to entirely disregard such, and that they had been 'sworn to give a true verdict'. Yet he must have been confident that, as he rested his case, he had demonstrated what was necessary for the jury to find Mary guilty. That she knew the true, sinister nature of the powders, having seen the detrimental effects upon Susannah and Ann, as well as on her father from its first administration; that she had concealed this truth from Dr Addington, and that she had attempted to destroy the remaining powders, as well as burning Cranstoun's letters, which, if her story were true, were her only means of confirming it. In addition, Mary's attempts to bribe the servants, and her statements to Mr Fisher and the reported conversation with Mr Lane at the Little Angel, all served to prove Mary's incrimination beyond all doubt, regardless of Cranstoun's culpability in the murder of her father:

'If, upon that evidence, she appears to be innocent, in God's name let her be acquitted; but if, upon that evidence, she appears to be guilty, I am sure you will do justice to the public, and acquit your own consciences.'

It did not take very long for the jury to 'acquit their consciences' after Judge Legge had reviewed the evidence. Reading from his careful notes, after some general remarks upon the atrocity of the crime, and the nature and weight of circumstantial evidence 'more convincing and satisfactory than any other kind of evidence, because facts cannot lie', Legge reiterated that it was undeniable that Francis Blandy had died as a direct consequence of poison being administered to him by the prisoner at the bar. Nevertheless, he reminded the jury that 'What you are to try is reduced to this single question, whether the prisoner, at the time she gave it to her father, knew that it was poison, and what effect it would have?'

The jury, without retiring, consulted for five minutes and returned a verdict of guilty. After advising Mary 'to make the best and wisest use of the little time you are likely to continue in this world' Judge Legge placed the black cloth sentencing cap over his powdered wig and proceeded to pass sentence of death on Mary:

'That you are to be carried to the place of execution and there hanged by the neck until you are dead; and may God, of His infinite mercy, receive your soul.'

It was nine o'clock at night. The trial had lasted thirteen long hours. Mary rose for the last time to address the judge and the court. It was at this point, had she decided to sacrifice her good name, that Mary could have exercised a right which could have afforded her a stay of execution, namely the opportunity of 'pleading her belly'. Had she not been concerned with preserving the perception of her virtue, this last resort was a contrivance frequently exploited by many women who found themselves in similarly damning circumstances. Under English common law 'pleading the belly' permitted women in the later stages of pregnancy to be reprieved of their death sentences until after the delivery of the child. While the plea did not constitute a defence and could only be made after a guilty verdict had been passed, suffice to say such a successful plea nevertheless extended the life expectancy of the condemned mother-to-be, and in some instances, in the interim before the child was delivered in prison, a pardon could sometimes be secured, so it was clearly a more than worthwhile ploy. During the first quarter of the eighteenth century, at the Old Bailey alone, thirty-eight percent of the women sentenced to death aged between twelve and fifty years old entered such a plea during that period – on one occasion, four women found guilty in a single hearing all claimed they were pregnant. In such instances, verification of the claimant's condition was determined by what was termed as a 'jury of matrons', customarily drawn from women observing the proceedings in the courtroom, deemed to be experienced in such matters. If found to be 'quick with child', that is, on physical examination, the movements of the foetus could be detected, a reprieve would be granted until after the birth; no pregnant woman could be executed, as in doing so the life of the innocent party would be terminated along with the guilty mother. After the child was born the sentence of death was however reinstated.

Mary could have entered such a plea – after all, according to salacious gossip she had supposedly enjoyed the attentions of the Keeper's son – in the hopes of buying herself a little more precious time for the necessary application for clemency. Though she was not expecting a child, not all matronly examinations were conclusive, and besides 'pleading the belly' was a judicial reprieve that was open to abuse, causing one eighteenth-century commentator to complain that female felons would often have 'Matrons of [their] own Profession ready at hand, who, right or wrong, bring their wicked Companions quick with Child to the great Impediment of Justice'. In Daniel Defoe's novel *Moll Flanders*, written in 1721, one character successfully pleads her belly despite being 'no more with child than the judge that tried [her]'. But as matters stood, betraying no sign of

the fear, anguish or agitation that she might have been feeling, Mary only
asked that:

> 'as your lordship has been so good to show so much candour and
> impartiality in the course of my trial, I have one favour more to beg;
> which is, that your lordship would please to allow me a little time
> till I can settle my affairs and make my peace with God.'

Judge Legge, noted for his impartiality and humanity in his treatment of the
accused, gently replied, 'To be sure, you shall have a proper time allowed
you.'

In fact, Mary was to have a little more time to 'settle her affairs' than
anticipated. Though the date set for her execution was Saturday 4 April, the
University authorities objected on the grounds that it would be 'improper
and unprecedented' for a hanging to take place during the Holy Week of
Easter; the date of the execution was therefore postponed to the following
Monday – affording Mary a further two days of earthly existence.

Chapter 9

'...the whole published for the satisfaction of the publick'

The myriad reports featured in the publications, pamphlets and press, which the jury at Mary's trial had been assiduously directed to disregard, were just the tip of the iceberg. After her conviction, Mary was to prove newsworthy for months to come, indeed for the best part of 1752 and beyond; it was said that 'the pamphleteers kept the discussion alive a year longer than its subject'. One on-the-spot eighteenth century reporter, ready and waiting to capture the mood as Mary left Divinity Hall, noted in his account of her departure that 'she stepped into the Coach with as little Concern as if she had been going to a Ball'. Clearly, he was hoping for a rather more dramatic reaction to sensationalise his copy.

It is said that bad news travels the fastest, and in Mary's case word of her verdict preceded her return to Oxford Gaol. Whether the Keeper's family had become attached to Mary over the course of her remand (she had been lodged at Oxford Castle since the previous August after all) or they were firm adherents to her innocence, they were obviously affected by the verdict as when Mary arrived she found them 'in some Disorder, the Children being all in Tears'. Mary was nevertheless dismissive of her situation, saying 'Don't mind it,' adding 'What does it signify?' Apparently unperturbed by the court's judgement and the death sentence that she now faced, she said that she was 'very hungry' and asked to 'have something for supper as speedily as possible'. Mary's undiminished appetite was satisfied with 'Mutton Chops and an Apple Pye'.

During the almost five-week interim between her conviction and execution, as well as settling her affairs and making her 'peace with God' Mary utilised her time in penning a rebuttal to all those slight-worthy publications already in circulation, and the numerous opinions and accounts of her trial appearing in the popular press and periodicals of the day, to which significant column space was devoted. Amongst them was a verbatim account of the proceedings printed in *The Gentleman's Magazine*, a popular monthly magazine of its day featuring articles of news and commentary, as well as a sprinkling of satire, 'Taken in court with permission' and 'printed under the inspection of the judges'. Appearing on the same page as the report of the trial, in the listings for 'books published in April 1752' were three publications already available, each priced at 6d, detailing Mary's life and misdemeanours. The list would grow. In Horace Bleackley's *Some Distinguished Victims of the Scaffold*, published in 1905, the author, who included Mary Blandy in his 'selection from the dozen or more *causes célèbres* that stand out in special prominence', was careful to include in his bibliography no less than thirty 'contemporary tracts' pertaining to Mary's case, and amongst the bibliography which Bleackley so assiduously compiled, *An Authentic Narrative of that Most Horrid Parricide*, and *The Secret History of Miss Blandy* give an idea of just two of the catchy titles available.

Of course, the references made to Mary's case by later writers have added not inconsiderably to the list, as personified by William Roughead's comment in the preface to his 1914 *Trial of Mary Blandy*, that, 'Few cases in our criminal annals have occasioned a literature so extensive', and to which this publication must now be added. Despite this ever-increasing literary list, however, Mary's case inspired some dramatic and poetical interpretations as well; a sympathetic theatricalisation of Mary's plight, *The Fair Parricide* 'A Tragedy of Three Acts. Founded on a late melancholy event', appeared in May 1752, priced at one shilling, some poignant lines from which ran:

> 'Guilty or guiltless, who can surely tell?
> A spotless Angel, or a Fiend of Hell?
> To heaven alone we'll leave her dubious Case,
> And strive to mend the World through her Disgrace.'

Mary was again later memorialised as something of a tragic heroine in the 1827 poem *Henley*:

> 'Alas! the record of her page will tell
> That one thus madden'd, lov'd, and guilty fell.
> Who hath not heard of Blandy's fatal fame,
> Deplored her fate, and sorrowed o'er her shame?'

While poets and playwrights might have sorrowed over Mary's shame, and posited that her case would be best decided in the Kingdom to come, one of God's earthly representatives was nevertheless of a different mind. Four days after her trial, on 7 March, 'a Reverend Divine of Henley-upon-Thames', in all likelihood the Reverend William Stockwood, rector of the parish of Henley who had ministered to the spiritual needs of Francis Blandy in his last hours, addressed a letter to Mary, exhorting her to confession and repentance. The Reverend Divine opened his letter with:

'Had it been at my own option, I never would have chose to be the least concerned in your unhappy affair; but since divine providence, without my own seeking, has thought fit to order it otherwise, I shall, from obligations of compassion and humanity, offer some things to your serious consideration.'

He continued that as her life was 'forfeited to justice', 'May God grant that the fate of your soul may not resemble the fate of your body.' Spiritually comforting words indeed!

Mary responded to the Reverend with a letter of her own, clearly penned after due consideration on 9 March, in which she maintained that she had acted innocently, and while she 'never denied' that she was 'the fatal instrument' of her father's death she nevertheless 'knew not the nature of, nor had a thought those powders could hurt'. Furthermore, had she not destroyed Cranstoun's letters, as 'he commanded' everyone would have been convinced that she had no intention 'to kill or hurt my poor father; I hope God will forgive me'. In the same letter Mary also begged that the Reverend be so kind as to pass on her 'tenderest wishes' to her godmother, Mrs Mounteney, who had been so affected by giving evidence for the prosecution against Mary, and likewise to her former suitor; 'Pray comfort poor Ned Hearne [sic], and tell him I have the same friendship for him as ever.' Mary also alluded to Mrs Mounteney's being able to 'serve' her with regard to an application for a reprieve, to be addressed to the Bishop of Winchester, her expectant yet misplaced hopes for clemency resting with the recently bereaved Princess Augusta, occasioned by the fact that she had once been singled out for the honour of dancing with the late Prince of Wales. There was a postscript:

'I beg, for very just reasons to myself and friends, that this letter and papers may soon be returned to me; that is, as soon as you have done with them. You will oblige me, if you keep a copy of the letter; but the real letter I would have back, and the real papers, as being my own handwriting, and may be of service to me, to my character after my death, and to my family.'

The 'real papers' referred to by Mary were, in fact, a narrative of her 'misfortunes'. Openly addressed to 'O! Christian Reader!', her own relation of the circumstances surrounding the crime for which she now stood condemned was the precursor to her subsequent, rather more lengthy narrative – in title as well as content – *Miss Mary Blandy's own account of the affair between her and Mr. Cranstoun, from the commencement of their acquaintance in the year 1746 to the death of her father in August, 1751, with all the circumstances leading to that unhappy event*. Witnessed by her own hand 'Signed by Miss Mary Blandy, in the Castle at Oxford, April 4, 1752, in presence of two Clergymen, members of the University of Oxford', Mary may well have been assisted in the compilation of her *Own Account* by the Reverend Swinton, the prison chaplain. This more than 14,000 word defence, described by Horace Bleackley as 'The most famous apologia in criminal literature' appeared in print on 18 April, just shy of a fortnight after Mary's execution. As the title indicated the account commenced from the time of Mary's first acquaintance with Cranstoun, back in the summer of 1746, and detailing the whole affair concluded with the entreaty that:

> 'The foregoing narrative, which I most earnestly desire may be published, was partly dictated and partly wrote by me, whilst under sentence of death; and is strictly agreeable to truth in every particular.'

Needless to say, a swift rejoinder appeared in the publication of *A Candid Appeal to the Publick* penned by 'a Gentleman of Oxford,' wherein 'All the ridiculous and false Assertions' contained in Mary's *Own Account* were 'exploded, and the Whole of that Mysterious Affair set in a True Light'.

Incredibly this 'Oxford Gentleman' was not alone amongst those who were Cranstoun's polemicists. Perhaps in a nod to a fellow countryman, both William Anderson and the Scottish historian T.F. Henderson were to vindicate Cranstoun; Anderson in his *The Scottish Nation* (1867) stated that 'There does not appear to have been any grounds for supposing that the captain was in any way accessory to the murder' while Henderson's entry for Cranstoun in the 1888 edition of the Oxford Dictionary of National Biography included his opinion that 'Apart from her [Mary Blandy's] statement there was nothing to connect him [Cranstoun] with the murder'.

Mary's own literary endeavours were not limited to her own exoneration, however, as while she awaited execution in Oxford Gaol she corresponded with various people, including another woman under sentence of death,

Elizabeth Jeffries. Jeffries had aided and abetted in the murder of her uncle, her lover John Swan was convicted along with her, and both were hanged at Epping Forest in Essex on the 28 March 1752. Another high-profile case of its day, when Mary became aware of Elizabeth's circumstances she commented:

> 'It is barbarous...for, in truth, the murder was a sordid business, and sadly lacking in "style"—but I am sorry for her, and hope she will have a good divine to attend her in her last moments, if possible a second Swinton, for, poor unhappy girl, I pity her.'

Permitted to write to one another while both awaited trial and execution, the ensuing correspondence between Mary and Elizabeth, dating from 7 January to 19 March 1752, made for another popular publication, entitled *Genuine Letters between Miss Blandy and Miss Jeffries, Before and After Conviction*. In these letters, both women protested their innocence to each other, and though Mary was to maintain her denial of ultimate culpability to the end, Elizabeth did later acknowledge her guilt to Mary. In her last letter to Elizabeth, dated 16 March, twelve days before Jeffries' joint execution with Swan, Mary reportedly wrote:

> 'Your deceiving of me was a small crime; it was deceiving yourself: for no retreat, tho' ever so pleasant, no diversions, no company, no, not Heaven itself, could have made you happy with those crimes un-repented of in your breast.'

Mary ended with the promise to be 'a suitor for her at the Throne of Mercy'; she would, after all, be hanged herself nine days later. Mary's strictures aside, she was nevertheless affronted to hear that one of her visitors, who regarded Jeffries as a common criminal and deserving of her fate, had been shocked to learn that Mary herself was sympathetic to Elizabeth's plight. To this visitor's sanctimonious attitude, Mary was on record as having said, 'I can't bear these over virtuous women. I believe that if ever the devil picks a bone it is one of theirs.'

Though the age of dissembling moral principle was yet to reach its zenith in the Victorian era, Mary's censorious visitor might be excused for her condemnation of any empathy felt for Elizabeth Jeffries, as she was indeed the cold-blooded instigator of her uncle's murder. In mitigation, however, though it was commonly held that she shared Cranstoun's motive, that is money, for she stood to inherit a fortune, there were nevertheless rumours that Elizabeth had been the victim of sexual assault, at the hands of her uncle, from a very young age, culminating in his raping her at the age of 15. Certainly, Horace Walpole, the eminent Whig politician and gossip, acknowledged the possibility; in a letter written to a friend on 23rd March 1752, he commented:

'There are two wretched women that just now are as much talked of... a Miss Jefferies [sic] and a Miss Blandy; the one condemned for murdering her uncle, the other her father. Both their stories have horrid circumstances; the first having been debauched by her uncle; the other had so tender a parent, that his whole concern while he was expiring, and knew her for his murderess, was to save her life.'

Mary herself must have been acquainted with the full background to Elizabeth's case. That her uncle, Joseph Jeffries, a wealthy, childless man who lived in Walthamstow, Essex, had adopted Elizabeth as his niece when she was just five years old. Though his will was made in her favour, her uncle threatened to change it, supposedly because of Elizabeth's rebellious teenage behaviour; however, if the allegations of abuse were founded, his threats of disinheritance may well have been intended to ensure Elizabeth's submission to his continued perversions, which had she refused would have seen her left on the streets and destitute. No surprise then that by the time she had turned twenty-one, Elizabeth had been contemplating her uncle's murder for some two years. The only problem was that she could not see a way of accomplishing the deed unaided. Driven by the increasing likelihood of her disinheritance, Elizabeth decided to enlist the assistance of her uncle's gardener, John Swan, with whom she was supposed to have been 'intimate'. Their plan to involve a third party, a former servant of Mr Jeffries' named Matthews, was to prove a mistake, however. In spite of the share of the inheritance which Matthews was offered as blood money, the staged robbery during which Matthews was supposed to shoot Joseph Jeffries went awry. When it came to it, Matthews was unable to bring himself to go through with the deed, so Swan finished the job himself. As Mr Jeffries was supposed to have been shot by an intruder, with no sign of any apparent forced entry, the authorities went ahead and arrested Elizabeth in view of her pecuniary motive. However, when no evidence could be produced against her, Elizabeth was released, but not before she had implicated Matthews. This was to be her undoing. Her liberty to enjoy her inheritance was cut short when Matthews was tracked down and gave a full account of the murder, turning King's evidence and saving his own neck. Elizabeth was promptly re-arrested, along with Swan, and both were committed to Chelmsford prison to await trial at the next Assizes.

When she was found guilty, Elizabeth, not sharing in the fortitude that Mary Blandy had exhibited at her trial, fainted as the sentence of death was pronounced. At her and Swan's joint execution, as she was of small stature, Elizabeth was made to stand on a chair and fainted several times as she was being prepared to meet her Maker. As was noticeable with other couples in their situation, any notions of love or romance had long since evaporated by the time the gallows loomed. Elizabeth and John did not communicate with one another at all, not even by a glance. While Swan died in less than five minutes, Elizabeth, being lighter than Swan, took over fifteen minutes to hang, struggling to the end.

Though Elizabeth Jeffries' murderous intent, for whatever motive, was clear from the outset, other parallels, beside her and Mary's congruent fates were apparent. Both Elizabeth Jeffries and Mary Blandy were middle-class women cut from the finer cloth of society's fabric; hailing from respectable backgrounds, raised in relative comfort, both had received at least a reasonable education. As such, and reflecting contemporary societal attitudes, both were a departure from those women born of the eighteenth underclass whose assumed widespread criminality was the product of poverty and social inequality, the hardships and tensions they suffered the drivers for those convicted of whoring, often in league with pickpockets, and petty theft before progressing on to further serious crime. While such women were generally unlikely to perpetrate a violent crime, when they did it was more often than not restricted to the familial sphere, the murder of a spouse for example, or in the face of dire deprivation, reduced to the miserable extreme of smothering their own children at birth.

With regards to their sex, Elizabeth and Mary were also at a disadvantage. Any woman who killed her husband, father, or step-uncle for that matter, was held to have broken the 'natural hierarchy', effectively straying from the path of traditional femininity, and striking at the very principles of the then perceived patriarchal social structure. This prevalent attitude was amply reflected in the prejudicial view taken of female felons by the judiciary at the time; female offenders were more likely to be stigmatised, having compounded their legal transgressions by compromising their idealised roles as mothers and obedient wives and daughters. Before either Mary or Elizabeth had even set foot in the courtroom, their crimes had been 'gendered', weighed against the ideal of societal conformity, their prosecution viewed as a moral triumph for society at large. Added to which, the cultural fear of female criminality was indelibly stamped on the collective psyche. Masculine authority and patriarchal familial order were the foundation upon which eighteenth-century society was built, born of centuries of female subjugation, and the 'deviant' criminality of women such as Mary and Elizabeth posed a threat to that masculine authority, not to mention their flouting of the respect due to their elders. The firm guiding hand of a husband or father was seen as an unquestionable necessity, and absolute obedience and deference was fundamental, instilled from the earliest age and supposedly extended to even the most wilful of daughters, and, of course, adopted nieces. Consequently, it was the murder of kin that weighed the heaviest of all, the destruction of the family from within a highly threatening prospect in a society dependent on strong ties of kinship. Compounding the crime, in Elizabeth's case, she would also have been branded a 'Jezabel', Swan seduced into becoming her accomplice with the lure of sexual favours, though, if she had in fact done so, in Georgian society she would have had scant other means of persuasion at her disposal.

Concerning Mary's place in this restricted society, as a female, she also did nothing to diminish the stereotype of the poisoning woman, a pernicious stock character throughout history. To this day, the pervasive view taken of a poisoner is that they could never claim that the crime was committed in the 'heat of the moment', in the throes of a *crime passionnel*, or driven by the compulsions of a psychopath, and this somehow makes the act seem controlled, premeditated and all the more sinister. When he spoke for the prosecution at Mary's trial, Mr Serjeant Hayward expressed his own horror of the deed. 'Of all kinds of murders that by poison is the most dreadful, as it takes a man unguarded, and gives him no opportunity to defend himself'. Seen as a method of murder frequently employed by females – 'poison is a woman's weapon' – since antiquity, women were the guardians of the domestic realm and the keepers of the keys to the kitchen cabinets. The lady of the house was also ideally placed to conveniently administer a poison as she was predominantly involved with the preparation of food and the management of and access to household remedies and 'medicines'. Governed by a skill set requiring no physical effort, and a crime that could be committed by stealth and in private, behind closed doors and with no direct witnesses, pertinent to Cranstoun's intent, death by poison can surely be accomplished at a distance as on the spot.

After setting Mary on her murderous path, Cranstoun had certainly succeeded in distancing himself. After his flight to the Continent, in his absence, the War Office had wasted no time in instructing the Paymaster-General to strike Cranstoun's name from the half-pay list, he having been 'charg'd with contriving the manner of sd. Miss Blandy's Poisoning her Father and being an Abettor therein: And he having absconded from the time of her being comitted [sic] for the above Fact'.

As for Cranstoun's apprehension, after the botched efforts and the debacle in securing the arrest warrant in Scotland, on 4 October the Lord Chancellor had written to the Secretary of State regarding a petition by the 'Noblemen and Gentlemen in the Neighbourhood of Henley-upon-Thames, and the Mayor and principal Magistrates of that Town' that in order to bring to justice 'the Wicked Contriver and Instigator of this Villainous Scheme,' His Majesty might be pleased to offer by proclamation a reward for Cranstoun's capture. While there was general approval for putting a price on Cranstoun's head, the action seemed futile as by then it was thought probable that by now he would 'be gone beyond sea'. The supposition was, of course, correct; Cranstoun had been in France since early September. His assumed absence, however, did not prevent what remains a pernicious nuisance to this day – then as now, high-profile cases attracting publicity are also likely to attract hoaxers. Criminal hoaxing is often motivated by an individual's perceived capacity to influence events, yet malicious intent is nevertheless frequently the hallmark of the hoaxer, and certainly, this must have been the motive behind the penning of the threatening letter received by Betty Binfield. Purporting to have been written by Cranstoun, the inference was that he was still in the country, a fugitive lying concealed 'either here in London or in the North'. The notion was hastily dismissed, however, as was the further 'menacing letter', signed with Cranstoun's initials, 'W.H.C.', which had been received by Dr Lewis, Addington's associate, on 23 November.

Whether it was the same sad fantasist, anxious for association with the publicity surrounding Mary's case, who had written both letters, they must have been deluded if they thought to convince the authorities that Cranstoun was still in the country; he would indeed have been short-sighted if he were to so commit himself. In reality, after a short stay in the Calais lodgings which Francis Gropptty had arranged for him, Cranstoun moved on to Boulogne. A shrewd decision, as to stay in one place for too long would have increased the risk of his discovery, and besides, in Boulogne Cranstoun could avail himself of the hospitality of a distant family relative, a Mrs Ross, who lived there. Ever the consummate con-artist, Cranstoun must have been convincing when he told Mrs Ross his own version of the events leading up to his arrival in France. Imploring her to take pity on him, and conceal him until 'the storm was a little blown over', Mrs Ross agreed to harbour the kindred fugitive, but proposed that it would be expedient if Cranstoun were to go by another name, suggesting he adopt her maiden name – Dunbar – instead of his own. Though he thought he was safe, for the time being at least, unfortunately for Cranstoun, fate was to play its hand; he was not the only one who had relatives in Boulogne. Some relatives of Anne Murray (Mrs Anne Cranstoun), were officers in a French regiment, currently billeted in the town. Though he had adopted a false identity, and doubtless disguised his appearance, exposure was still a possibility, and fearing the inevitable reprisals, not to mention the probability of arrest, Cranstoun confined himself to Mrs Ross's house, where he remained holed up until 26 July. One has to wonder, in his solitary moments, whether he gave any thought to Mary, who had been executed more than three months before.

Though Cranstoun was fully aware of the risk, unable to stand his self-imposed confinement any longer, and still fearful that his hiding place would eventually be revealed, after consultation with Mrs Ross, who, unless she was of a very hospitable nature must have been equally exacerbated by the duration of the enforced residence of her house-guest, Cranstoun decided to move on to Paris. A horse-drawn stagecoach would have made the journey from Boulogne to the French capital inside of a long, dusty day – highwaymen and the state of the roads permitting that is, but Cranstoun opted to go on foot instead, lest his hiring a carriage or travelling in a public coach attract unwanted attention. He was also careful to break his journey overnight in obscure village inns along the way. In the meantime, while Cranstoun was tramping across the French countryside, Mrs Ross was to go to Furnes, a town across the border in Flanders, and secure suitable lodgings for her kinsman there – the travel and accommodation costs presumably met at her own expense, as after only a fortnight in Paris, Cranstoun's funds had virtually dried up.

Setting out for Furnes (as the distance involved was in excess of 180 miles, Cranstoun may well have risked the exposure of travelling by coach, if only for part of the journey) when he arrived, the lodgings arranged by the obliging Mrs Ross were 'at the sign of the Burgundy Cross'. However, not long after his arrival in Flanders, Cranstoun was taken with a severe 'Fit of Illness'. Some might say that this was a divine retribution – indeed the state of Cranstoun's health occasioned his abandonment of his former

Presbyterian faith and his conversion to Catholicism, smacking of hypocrisy in view of the pressures he admitted having brought to bear on his lawful wife to convert from that faith herself. Cranstoun's suffering was to last for nine days, though over the course of the last three days 'his pains were so very great, and he was swelled to such a degree, that it was thought by the physician and apothecary that attended him, that he would have burst, and by the great agonies he expired in, he was thought to be raving mad'. The fact that Cranstoun suffered 'great agonies' before death was noted by one of his less than sympathetic biographers as 'satisfactory'! It would seem from his symptoms that Cranstoun was suffering from 'dropsy', the archaic term for oedema, a build-up of fluid in the body, and symptomatic of heart failure, or impairment of liver or kidney function. Aged thirty-nine or thereabouts, while by today's standards Cranstoun would have been regarded as relatively young for such a diagnosis, his swelling 'to such a degree' would suggest cardiac dropsy, now called congestive heart failure, which also limits kidney function. Without treatment, the resultant swelling, initially to the ankles, progresses further up the body until the heart fails completely, or develops an irregular beat and the patient dies. Digitalis, obtained from the dried leaves of the common foxglove, would eventually prove an effective treatment. However, the first prescribed use of the drug in 1785 came far too late to alleviate Cranstoun's agonies. His afflictions were such that he 'felt such Torments… as made him wish for Death for some days before he died', which he did on 30 November 1752. The Honourable William Henry Cranstoun had outlived Mary by a little less than eight months. At his end, in moments of lucidity, did he draw any consolation from the fact that his passing was in a bed rather than at the end of a rope?

After his death, Cranstoun's personal belongings, 'consisting chiefly of Laced and Embroidered Waistcoats,' were sold to pay off his debts. Buried in accordance with the rights of his newly embraced faith 'a grand Mass was said over the corpse in the Cathedral Church, which, was finely illuminated'. The town's dignitaries even turned out to pay their respects, 'in great solemnity, the Corporation attending the funeral'. Whether they would have done so had they been acquainted with Cranstoun's true circumstances is another matter, his body may very well have been unceremoniously heaved into a pauper's grave.

Shortly before he died, Cranstoun had drawn up his will, which was sealed in the presence of Mrs Ross and two other people, who were also his acquaintances, and signed in his own name, rather than under his 'Dunbar' pseudonym. His last bequest was that all his fortune, which was in his brother's hands, be made over to his daughter, who was now living in Hexham in Northumberland, with her mother, to whom the now contrite Cranstoun admitted having 'so villainously denied being married'. Cranstoun added that he was of the belief that 'a curse had attended him for injuring the character of so good a wife'. With regard to any last thoughts of Mary, Cranstoun made a dying declaration that 'he and Miss Blandy were privately married before the death of her mother, which was near on two years before Mr Blandy was poisoned'. Whether or not he was prepared to die with a lie on his lips, in his last confession, when Francis Blandy's murder was touched upon, Cranstoun said that 'Miss Blandy ought not to have blamed him so much as she did, but the particulars of which... should never be known till his death'. Possibly Cranstoun was making reference to the accountability he would face when judged in the celestial courts of the 'great Hereafter', or it might have been that he had left a written admission of his guilt, to be opened after his death. Either way, after the funeral a letter was sent to his mother, the Dowager Lady Cranstoun, to which she replied with instructions that all of her son's papers 'of every kind' be sealed up and secured. These were then to be sent to his brother, Lord Cranstoun in Scotland. While Lady Cranstoun's intention must have been to preserve the confidentiality of her son's papers, and ameliorate the tarnish attached to the Cranstoun family name, the inevitable publications nevertheless appeared. The *Memories of the life and most remarkable transactions of Capt. William Henry Cranstoun* was published within a year of his death; this was just the precursors of many more accounts, numbering amongst at least four biographies that were to follow.

The validity of these accounts, then, as now, is left to the judgement of the reader, but *Captain Cranstoun's Account of the Poisoning of the late Mr. Francis Blandy* which was intended as a counterblast to Mary's *Own Account* must be held in an obviously dubious light. In this particular account of 'Mr. Cranstoun's distresses', 'declared solemnly by him before he died at Furnes in Flanders', as well as alluding to the 'particulars of his private marriage with the late unfortunate Miss Blandy' she having 'desired and insisted it should be so, and was very pressing till it was done', the text of three letters, alleged to have been written by Mary to Cranstoun also appeared, having been 'found immediately after his Decease, in his Portmanteau-Trunk in his Room'. Conveniently these missives set 'that whole tragical affair in a true light', that Mary was 'fully resolved' on poisoning her father, and that Cranstoun 'often called upon God Almighty to forgive both his Crimes, and those of Miss Blandy', but 'particularly' Mary's, 'as she had died with asserting so many enormous Falsities', against Cranstoun, those contained in her *Own Account*.

We can assume that the defensive accounts of Cranstoun's involvement in the murder of Francis Blandy were read with the same alacrity as those of a derogatory nature written about Mary, '... the whole published for the satisfaction of the publick'. Indeed that same 'publick' doubtless eagerly purchased the broadside produced by Pitts Printers in Seven Dials entitled *Execution of Miss Blandy*, their collective morbid fascination satisfied by the relation of some poignant aspects of Mary's final moments, which would later pass into legend.

Chapter 10

A Very Modest Murderess

'For the sake of decency, Gentlemen, don't hang me high.'
Mary Blandy, Monday 6th April 1752

M ary's execution drew near, though as we shall see, her story in no
way ended with her death.

The reason for the postponement of Mary's execution, originally
set for Saturday 4 April, was at the request of the University authorities, who
took the view that a hanging during Holy Week would be ungodly, 'improper
and unprecedented'. While the *when* was settled, there does, however, seems to
be some difference of opinion with regards to *where* Mary Blandy was executed.
In the eighteenth century, every county had a place of execution, normally at or
near the county (Assize) town. However, in some towns, there were two places
set aside for public execution, as at Oxford, where hangings could take place
either in the Castle Yard, which was, in fact, a large open space, or at the gallows
set up on a raised mound just outside the West Gate of the city. The mound
or 'motte' is the main surviving part of Oxford's original Norman castle, built
after the Conquest. According to one account, on the night before her execution
Mary is supposed to have asked to see where she would be hanged the next day;
looking out from one of the upper windows she could see the makeshift gallows
'opposite the door of the gaol,' which had been improvised 'by laying a poll [sic]
across upon the arms of two trees'. Mary turned away, supposedly remarking
that it was 'very high'. Her concerns over the loftiness of the makeshift gallows
will later become clear. But in another account, it was reported that a rumour
had been circulated that Mary was to be hanged on the Friday before the 6th,
from the West Gate gallows, and as word spread 'a very great concourse of people
were got together upon the Castle Green, to be spectators of the execution'.
Mary is said to have looked out several times upon this throng from the room
facing the Green, commenting that 'she would not balk their expectations, tho'
her execution might be deferred a day or two longer'.

There is a contemporary engraving by Benjamin Cole, who was clearly
a master of many trades, a surveyor, cartographer, instrument maker,
bookbinder and engraver living in Oxford at the time, entitled *Miss*

Mary Blandy, with scene of her Execution. Beneath the larger image of a fashionably dressed Mary, holding a flower between the fingers of her left hand, Cole included a smaller depiction of her lifeless body, dangling from a crudely-improvised gallows, a wooden pole, or beam, wedged between the branches of two trees approximately ten feet apart. Beyond the throng of spectators, a doorway and a window of the castle building can be made out. *The new and complete Newgate Calendar*, published in 1795, 'Illustrated with upwards of sixty most elegant copper plates' includes the image of Mary ascending the ladder to a conventional three-sided gallows, in the background the castle mound and the distant buildings of the city clearly visible. However, as this edition of *The Newgate Calendar* was compiled more than forty years after Mary's execution, and as Cole's engraving would seem to be near on contemporary, the pictorial evidence is suggestive that Mary was in fact hanged in Oxford's Castle-yard, and moreover supported by the written contemporary accounts of her final hours.

The day before her execution, Mary had received the Holy Sacrament, and also wrote and signed the following statement in a last protestation of her innocence:

'I, Mary Blandy, do declare, that I die in a full persuasion of the truth and excellency of the Christian religion, and a sincere, though unworthy, member of the Church of England. I do likewise hope for a pardon and remission of my sins, by the mercy of God, through the merits and mediation of Jesus Christ, my most blessed Lord and Saviour. I do also further declare, that I did not know or believe that the powder, to which the death of my dear father has been ascribed, had any noxious or poisonous quality lodged in it; and that I had no intention to hurt, and much less to destroy him, by giving him that powder; All this is true, as I hope for eternal salvation, and mercy from Almighty God, in whose most awful and immediate presence I must soon appear. I die in perfect peace and charity with all mankind and do from the bottom of my soul forgive all my enemies, and particularly those who have in any manner contributed to or been instrumental in bringing me to the ignominous [sic] death I am so soon to suffer. This is my last declaration, as to the points therein contained; and I do most earnestly desire, that it may be published after my decease. Witness my hand, MARY BLANDY.'

The night before her execution, Sunday 5 April, Mary spent mostly in prayer. She went to bed at her usual time, and though she had requested that she not be woken until as late as possible the following morning, not to be disturbed before eight o'clock, understandably she had difficulty sleeping, and between three and four o'clock she was awake and praying in her bed, after which she gave up entirely on the idea of sleep and rose and dressed herself.

Accordingly, at about half-past eight on the morning of Monday 6 April, the Sheriff, accompanied by Mary's attorney, Mr Rivers, and the chaplain, the Reverend Swinton, arrived at the gaol. After half an hour spent in private contemplation with the chaplain, Mary was led out into the castle yard, where the sheriff's men and the executioner were waiting for her. Each county had a High Sheriff who was appointed for a year and had the responsibility, amongst other things, of carrying out the punishments ordered by the courts. In capital cases, it was the sheriff's responsibility to organise the execution and appoint the executioner from an approved list. The execution would proceed under the direction of the sheriff and went ahead irrespective of whether there might be the possibility of a reprieve, even at the last minute. It is unlikely that there was any such expectation in Mary's case, however, the hopes expressed in the previous chapter seemingly unrealistic, to say the least.

Sombrely attired as she had been for her trial, 'dress'd in a black crape sack', Mary's arms and hands were 'ty'd [sic] with black paduasoy ribbons', presumably a nod to her gentility, the 'paduasoy' ribbons made from heavy, rich corded silk were a refined substitute for harsh rope. In 1760, Laurence Shirley, 4th Earl Ferrers, the last peer to be hanged and the only peer to have been hanged for murder was executed at Tyburn; Ferrers reputedly met his fate at the end of a silken rope. While the Reverend Swinton read aloud several prayers deemed suitable for the occasion, Mary's courage did not falter, and in accordance with the custom of the day, she made her 'dying declaration'. Mary had been concerned that the sudden shock of seeing the gallows might render her unable to speak, however having had the opportunity to view her place of execution from one of the 'upper windows' of the castle, mentioned earlier, when the time came her spirits did not fail her.

'Good people,' she cried, in a clear, audible voice:

'give me leave to declare to you that I am perfectly innocent as to any intention to destroy or even hurt my dear father; that I did not know, or even suspect, that there was any poisonous quality in the fatal powder I gave him; though I can never be too much punished for being even the innocent cause of his death. As to my mother's and Mrs Pocock's deaths, that have been unjustly laid to my charge, I am not even the innocent cause of them, nor did I in the least contribute to them. So help me, God, in these my last moments. And may I not meet with eternal salvation, nor be acquitted by Almighty God, in whose awful presence I am instantly to appear hereafter, if the whole of what is here asserted is not true. I from the bottom of my soul forgive all those concerned in my prosecution; and particularly the jury, notwithstanding their fatal verdict.'

The two guineas she had held in her hand had already been paid to the hangman – it was customary for the condemned to pay their executioner to ensure a 'professional' service was rendered. A skilled hangman's knot would ensure the certainty of a broken neck, usually at the third vertebra below the skull, and therefore a swift end; the alternative was a slow and agonising death by strangulation. The sinister origin of the phrase 'to pull one's leg' and the expression 'hangers on' harks back to the time when a criminal's family would pay someone to pull down on their legs as they were hanged, thereby minimising their suffering. As Mary ascended the ladder, draped in black cloth for the occasion, after she had reached the fifth rung she faltered, and made her last, most memorable request, that 'for the sake of decency, gentlemen, don't hang me high'. Her modest concern that the young men in the crowd might be afforded a view up her skirts. While it was common to tie the legs of a female prisoner prior to their execution from a purpose-built scaffold, or 'drop', to ensure that their skirts would not billow up, exposing their underwear, or lack thereof – the wearing of underpants, or drawers, did not become commonplace until as late as the very end of the eighteenth century – as it was necessary for Mary to climb a ladder to reach the noose dangling from the makeshift gallows, this would have proved nigh on impossible had her legs been bound.

Asked to step up a little higher, Mary managed to climb two further rungs, before turning herself about and saying, 'I am afraid I shall fall.' Yet in a final show of courage and self-possession, she addressed the crowd one last time, 'Good people, take warning by me to be on your guard against the sallies of any irregular passion, and pray for me that I may be accepted at the Throne of Grace.' The hangman, confident that Mary's had ascended the ladder to a height that would ensure a sufficient drop, placed the noose around her neck, but as it touched her face, she was heard to give a deep sigh. Moving the noose to one side herself, Mary covered her face with a white handkerchief, however as it did not entirely cover her features, a female attendant stepped forward, and after adjusting the noose pulled the handkerchief down further. Though Mary's hands had been secured with the 'paduasoy ribbons' they had been tied in front of her body so that she could hold her prayer book, but also to allow her to signal that she was ready to die; it had been agreed beforehand that when she had finished her prayers, she would drop the prayer book as a sign to the hangman that she was ready to be 'turned off'. Accordingly, as the book hit the ground, the ladder was turned over and Mary Blandy was launched into eternity. It was reported that she passed into unconsciousness very quickly and 'died without a struggle'. The two guineas paid to the hangman was clearly money well spent. Horace Walpole was later to comment in a letter written to a friend that:

'Miss Blandy died with a coolness of courage that is astonishing, and denying the fact, which has made a kind of party in her favour; as if a woman who would not stick at parricide would scruple a lie!'

Ordinarily, for the populace at large, the spectacle of seeing a gentlewoman in the hands of the executioner was an opportunity not to be missed. Hanging days were holidays, often taking on a mass entertainment quality, and human nature being what it was – and some would say still is, in spite of contemporary society's supposed heightened sensibilities – these events turned out to be a perversely enjoyable distraction from the routine grind of everyday life. Crowds including families with young children would bring along a picnic and make a day of it, and despite the obvious taste and enthusiasm for the spectacle of a public execution, while the gruesome display was intended as a deterrent to crime and cold hard proof that justice had been served, rather than inspiring a dread silence, spectators were rather more inclined to give up a lusty cheer as the guilty dangled from the end of the rope. However, of the crowd gathered to watch Mary's execution – according to *A Complete Collection of State Trials*, compiled in 1816 – estimated 'at 5,000 strong', it was noted that the majority of those who attended were so affected by Mary's dignified behaviour that they 'fell to weeping', their sobs the only sound to be heard amidst the otherwise awestruck air of silence. While the heightened profile of Mary's case assured that her execution afforded for 'a great draw', while morbid fascination might have ruled the day, accounting for the multitudes of gaping onlookers running into thousands, all the same many went away that day convinced of her innocence.

After execution by hanging, it was usual for the body to be left dangling for about half an hour before being cut down and, ordinarily, claimed by friends or relatives for burial. In addition to prolonging the reproving spectacle of execution, this delay also ensured that condemned person was actually dead – in theory at least. While cheating the hangman's noose was an unusual occurrence to say the least, it was not unheard of. One such instance had occurred in Oxford in 1650, in the very same castle yard, when twenty-two-year-old Anne Green was hanged, albeit unsuccessfully. A domestic servant, Anne had been seduced by her master's grandson – young women in domestic service were particularly vulnerable to sexual harassment, especially at the hands of 'predatory' employers and their kin. Anne was subsequently convicted of infanticide after the discovery of her bastard child's corpse, hidden in her master's house, and though the child had been stillborn, infanticide was a crime for which a woman could be found guilty, under a statute passed in 1624, even if she simply tried to conceal her pregnancy and later miscarried, or if the infant was stillborn. The 'professional' service of a well-compensated hangman was not to be Anne's experience; her compassionate friends, desperate to limit her suffering pulled down 'with all their weight upon her leggs [sic]… lifting her up and then pulling her downe againe with a suddain [sic] jerke' in order to hasten the poor woman's death. Incredibly, in spite of the vigorous attempts to speed her to her end, after she was cut down, on being placed in her coffin, Anne was found to still have a pulse. After some hasty and rudimentary medical intervention, which included giving her a tobacco smoke enema, she fully recovered and was granted a reprieve and declared innocent. As a footnote to Anne's story, she later married and bore three healthy children, dying in her own bed in 1665, but she nevertheless kept her coffin as a souvenir!

While Mary's hanging had proceeded without incident, the post-execution arrangements were far from satisfactory. When the Sheriff gave the order for Mary's lifeless body, her feet almost touching the ground, to be cut down after the appointed time, it became apparent that the provision of a coffin had been overlooked, and that the order for a hearse to carry the body away had also been neglected. In the circumstances, one would have thought that the Sheriff, in the name of public decency, might have given instructions for Mary's corpse to be carried back into the castle, until such time as proper arrangements could be made. However, her body was instead unceremoniously slung over the shoulder of one of the Sheriff's men and carried 'in the most beastly manner' through the crowds; Mary's modest fears were realised, 'her legs exposed very indecently for several hundred yards'. After this posthumous humiliation, Mary's body was deposited in the house of her rough escort, there to await a hearse to take her back to Henley for burial, which eventually arrived at about half-past five that evening.

Mary's burial took place in the early hours of Tuesday morning, the 7 April, in the chancel of St Mary the Virgin, Henley's Parish Church, between the graves of her father and her mother. The church has since been restored, and while there is now no indication of the Blandy family grave, it is believed to be beneath the organ, in the north choir aisle. The entry made in the burial register for Mary's interment reads, 'Blandy, Mary' – and then in another hand and a different ink – 'was this day executed at Oxford for poisoning her father Mr Francis Blandy, Attorney'. Presumably this comment was added at the same time and by the same individual responsible for the later addition made to the entry for Francis Blandy's burial.

Despite the earliness of the hour, necessitated by haste and discretion; convicted criminals were not customarily buried within church bounds, 'there was assembled the greatest concourse of people ever known upon such an occasion', though Mary's funeral was still a far cry from the pretentious and elaborate solemnities afforded to Cranstoun when he came to be interred. The officiating clergyman was the Reverend William Stockwood, the presumed 'Reverend Divine of Henley-upon-Thames' who had written to Mary in gaol four days after her trial, 'exhorting her to confession and repentance'. Yet in spite of his admonishments, he was nevertheless one of the beneficiaries of Mary's last bequest, that being for seven guineas be set aside to purchase seven rings to be given out after her death. Mary was magnanimous enough to include the Reverend Stockwood amongst the seven beneficiaries.

Though Mary had suffered the posthumous indignity of bodily public exposure, the fear of which had been uppermost in her mind before her execution, her corpse was at least to be spared open desecration before an audience of medical students. In 1752 the 'Act for the better preventing the horrid Crime of Murder', more commonly known as the 'Murder Act', had been passed, mandating for the dissection of the bodies of all executed murderers, including females. As medical research grew so did the need for cadavers, and by the 1700's, in England, the limited number of bodies of selected executed criminals and the 'unclaimed poor' given over to feed the need of surgical teaching schools and hospitals proved insufficient. Some legislation was required, and the introduction of the Murder Act not only benefited the medical fraternity but also sharpened the deterrent effect of the death penalty, 'that some further terror and peculiar mark of infamy be added to the punishment', the sentence of dissection preying heavily on the very real dread felt by the majority of the population at the thought of dismemberment after death. There was a strong belief that dissection and the desecration of a deceased's body, rendering it incomplete, would prevent that individual's entry into Heaven. The Act also served to allay the government's concerns that too often the bodies of convicted murderers were accorded the dignity of a full funeral and buried in consecrated ground, a reprehensible entitlement in view of their crime, hence the inclusion of the provision that 'in no case whatsoever shall the body of any murderer be suffered to be buried'. The first body to be submitted for the posthumous fate of dissection after the 'Murder Act' came into force on the 1st June 1752, was that of seventeen-year-old Thomas Wilford. Found guilty of murdering his wife just one week after their wedding, Wilford had cut his bride's throat with such force 'that her head was almost severed from her body'. He was executed on 22 June 1752, and his body given over to the Surgeons' Company accordingly. If Mary Blandy had been hanged just eight weeks later, her body would likewise have been eligible for the same fate.

Though Mary's earthly existence had been terminated, it would seem that her spirit was far from quiet. Notwithstanding the poignant legend which grew up about a blackbird which had perched on the beam of the makeshift gallows during her execution – it is said that to this day no blackbird has ever sung in the vicinity – accounts of Mary's hauntings abound. Said to manifest at Oxford Castle, as well as at the gallows site next to the castle mound, now occupied by the redeveloped Westgate shopping centre, Mary supposedly still frequents her hometown of Henley. Seen beneath an old mulberry tree in the garden of the Blandy's old house on Hart Street, on occasion accompanied by the shadowy figure of a man, presumably the spectral Cranstoun, Mary's shadowy apparition has also been seen gliding about the town's streets, sometimes returning to her unmarked grave, but also making her presence felt at the Little Angel pub, where she had sought refuge from the angry mob who had pursued her over Henley Bridge. Mary has also been known to put in an appearance at the Red Lion Hotel, on Hart Street, where the night porter saw her wraith standing by a window. So that he would not forget what the apparition looked like, he drew a picture which he carried with him for two years, showing friends and acquaintances, before finally contacting the organiser of *Henley Ghost Tours*, the image now featured on their website. Appearing in another of Henley's hostelries, Mary's most recent manifestation was in the Catherine Wheel, also on Hart Street. Still newsworthy nearly two hundred and seventy years after her death, *The Henley Standard* wrote a feature article about the sighting, including the ethereal image of Mary in the bar, captured on a mobile phone.

Yet Mary has been known to stray a little further afield from time to time, her ghost said to walk the grounds of Park Place, across the Thames in Remenham, the scene of her assignations with Cranstoun, and which later became romantically known as 'Miss Blandy's Walk'. Over the years various sightings have been reported of a woman, apparently in 'fancy dress', wandering around the foot of Remenham Hill in the early hours of the morning, while the lanes around Turville and Hambleden also seem to be a favourite haunt of Mary's, stories about the ghost of a woman in 'old-fashioned clothes' being seen on Dolesden Lane near Turville, her dress rustling as she passes by. She's even been seen riding a white horse through Churchfield Woods, which border onto Turville Court, where she and her mother enjoyed the hospitality of Mrs Pocock, whom Mary was also accused of poisoning!

It would seem that after none of the Blandy family was left alive to occupy it, the empty old house on Hart Street acquired something of a sinister reputation of its own. Horace Walpole had himself taken a significant interest in Mary's case, and in a letter to a friend written on 4 August 1754, he related that:

> 'The town of Henley has been extremely disturbed with an engage-ment between the ghosts of Miss Blandy and her father, which continued so violent, that some bold persons, to prevent further bloodshed broke in and found it was two jackasses which had got into the kitchen.'

While eighteenth-century pranksters were responsible for the 'haunting' of the old Blandy home, Mary's restless shade was nevertheless held responsible for sparking the ghostly disturbances experienced at Henley's Kenton Theatre in 1969. Ranked as the fourth oldest working theatre in the country, the Kenton has a rich and varied past, but it was during the staging of Joan Morgan's *The Hanging Wood* that the paranormal phenomena occurred. Adapted from the novel of the same name, later retitled simply *Mary Blandy*, *The Hanging Wood* was written by Morgan in 1950, after the ex-silent screen star had retired to live in Henley and became acquainted with Mary's story. As soon as rehearsals began, so did the mysterious happenings. A large mirror was seen to literally jump off the wall of the dressing room, while the inexplicable knocks and bangs, lights switched on and off and doors opening and closing were the prelude to the phantom appearance of a young woman seen standing at the back of the theatre, watching the run-throughs. Nobody ever actually saw her arrive or leave the theatre for that matter, as when approached by a member of the cast, the figure simply disappeared. On another occasion, when several of the actors were discussing Mary Blandy during a break in rehearsals, a teacup was seen to rise from the table and drop to the floor, where it smashed to pieces. Was this Mary critiquing the theatrical versions of her own life story perhaps?!

'Dramatic' appearances aside, for those whose beliefs are firmly rooted in the corporeal plane, Mary still makes her presence felt through the pages of books, newspapers and indeed websites devoted to her crime, as well as her cause.

Chapter 11

A Contemporary Cause Célèbre

Much has been made of the matter of Mary's presumed guilt, and indeed the conjecture over her innocence; her case is one that still courts controversy today. While the reality of historical fact is inescapable, regardless of whether those facts are incomplete, wrong, distorted, or often too vague, human factors and the limitations of evidence can inhibit the discovery and presentation of a whole, unalloyed truth. The part played by interpretation and personal judgement, by prejudices and blind spots, in drawing a contemporary conclusion cannot, therefore, be underestimated, and all too often the desire to establish an unquestionable 'truth', in itself, unquestionably leads to a difference of opinion, and often a heated one at that. Amongst the more recent publications concerning Mary's case is that of Henley publisher Victor Bingham, *The Noose Around the Wrong Neck* squarely laying the blame for the murder of Francis Blandy on Cranstoun. However, Bingham's championing of Mary's cause was not restricted to the literary sphere, as in 2005 he made an application to the Criminal Cases Review Commission for Mary's conviction to be overturned. The Commission, set up in 1997, is an independent organisation, the principal role of which is to investigate suspected miscarriages of justice, and whose Commissioners take the important decisions about whether or not to send an applicant's case back to the courts for a fresh appeal. In light of the proposed appeal, Mary once again became newsworthy, providing further copy for *The Henley Standard*, the feature editor offering to pass along any public support from the people of Henley with regards to securing Mary's posthumous exoneration. Unfortunately, because of the age of the case, the application fell at the first hurdle, failing to meet the primary condition laid down when an appeal is made on behalf of one who is deceased. In accordance with the Criminal Appeal Act 1968, for an appeal to be heard in a case where the person involved has died, there has to be a relative deemed to have a close enough family connection to stand as their proxy in any appeal proceedings. The criteria of the Act effectively means that in a case which is almost 270 years old, the Court of Appeal would not give consideration to such an application in the absence of an individual with a sufficiently close familial connection. Consequently, for the Commission to review such a case would be futile. Besides which, such an action would divert resources from those cases of persons who are still alive and currently serving a prison sentence.

Touching on Mary's own hopes for a judicial reprieve through the agency of the Bishop of Winchester, and representation of her case to the Dowager Princess of Wales, at a time when capital convictions were fully realised, and remissions rare, though the grounds for appeal in the eighteenth century were very limited, the opportunity nevertheless existed, as did the prospect of a pardon. In the August of 1751, the month in which Francis Blandy died, such a pardon was granted when the murder conviction of Richard Coleman was overturned. Unfortunately for Coleman, he had already been hanged on 12 April 1749 for the crime which he had not committed. Amongst others, the execution of the innocent Richard Coleman demonstrates the flaws of capital punishment; while hanging was the favoured form of punishment for a capital crime, unlike a prison sentence, if the convicted person was wrongly accused, needless-to-say the penalty of hanging could not be reversed. Though the two men who had committed the crime for which Coleman had been executed were both eventually hanged in September 1751, the contemporary view nevertheless persisted that the execution of some innocent persons was simply the unavoidable cost of implementing capital punishment. Seen as a necessary government-sanctioned practice which not only acted as a deterrent, capital punishment also served to permanently remove the worst criminals from society; cold comfort however for the many who suffered as Coleman did, and possibly Mary Blandy.

Despite the abolition of the death penalty, with regards to historical factors affecting the process of criminal prosecution in today's legal system, Mary Blandy's case must be regarded as pivotal when considered as the turning point in the acceptance of detailed medical evidence in a court of law, a judicial milestone serving to highlight, in broader terms, the crucial contribution that the advancement in modern forensic understanding has had on the justice that is served today. Yet while the subsequent benefits of Dr Addington's efforts are beyond question, the path of decisive forensic testing applied to criminal proceedings has not always been a smooth one. After the Blandy trial, though the acceptance of medical testimony became more and more commonplace, its quality was nevertheless often questionable. Some practitioners had little idea of what to look for during an autopsy, never mind how to effectively apply toxicological tests, and invariably an unknown number of deaths were wrongly attributed to suicide and accident, and many poisonings were never detected; conversely, many wrongful convictions were made, as demonstrated by the case of Elizabeth Fenning.

In 1815 Elizabeth 'Eliza' Fenning was executed after being found guilty of the attempted poisoning of her employer, Robert Turner, along with his wife and his father, the delivery method a dinner of arsenic-laced dumplings. Popular opinion was largely in favour of Fenning's innocence, her case receiving much public attention, and at her funeral, as many as ten thousand people formed part of the procession to her grave. The arguments over Eliza's guilt were to continue for at least 20 years.

At her trial, as was usual at the time, the prosecution centred on Eliza's motive, opportunity and the general behaviour of the accused. When John Marshall, the family's physician, arrived, on finding the Turners, along with a housemaid and two apprentices, collapsed with violent stomach cramps and vomiting, he was convinced that the victims had been poisoned with white arsenic. The fact that Eliza herself was found slumped on the stairs, apparently in agony, was later put down to her having eaten a tiny portion of the poisoned dumplings in order to avoid suspicion. Witnesses were to testify that no one else had entered the kitchen while Eliza was preparing the dumplings, added to which that she seemed to dislike her employers and had failed to come to their aid, despite the fact that she was incapacitated herself. While this circumstantial evidence alone might have been enough to seal her fate and send Eliza to the gallows, there was also the added testimony of Dr Marshall in the capacity of 'expert' witness.

In 1815, the tests for the presence of arsenic were much as they were when Addington presented his findings at Mary Blandy's trial, and the fact remained that none of those tests was fool-proof. Regardless of the efficiency of the analysis carried out, however, Marshall made some serious procedural errors, and the neglected thoroughness of his examinations, coupled with his lack of knowledge concerning the chemical interactions and indicators of arsenic served to highlight the woeful inaccuracy of much of the specialist evidence presented to courts, particularly in poisoning cases. Nevertheless, upon such evidence many guilty verdicts were returned, as in Eliza's case, the courtroom accepting that the medical knowledge of professional practitioners was superior to that of the average person.

The reliance placed on the evidence of these so-called expert witnesses, who may or may not have been experts at all, more often than not merely the doctor attending the victim, would again be the determining factor in another contentious poisoning trial, six years after Eliza Fenning's, when Ann Barber stood accused of the murder of her husband in 1821. The autopsy on James Barber's body was carried out by the local apothecary-surgeon, James Hindle, who after analysing the stomach contents, announced that he was satisfied that the cause of death was arsenic poisoning, even going so far as to estimate the amount of poison administered. Hindle's misplaced confidence in his own skill as a pathologist was shockingly revealed however when, after discussing his findings in court, in what sounded like an expert manner, he offhandedly remarked that 'I never applied the test before and never saw any other person apply it. This poison is a subject I am very little acquainted with'. Incredibly the court paid no heed to Hindle's admission of his professional inadequacies; as was so often the case, the motive of the accused and details of their private lives were of more matter to a jury than any 'expert' testimony, regardless of its veracity. Needless to say, Ann was found guilty, and on her way to York's 'new drop' gallows, her 'shrieks were bitter and piercing, beyond anything that is possible to imagine… The heart-rending cries that announced her approach [to the scaffold] filled almost every face with dismay'.

While the convictions in both of these cases were clearly 'unsafe', it was Eliza Fenning's trial in particular, which, as well as garnering much public interest, also demanded academic attention, and in turn catalysed the further scientific developments in the field of forensics. The demand was made for doctors to be better trained in the newly developing scientific field, and at the spearhead of this campaign was a former Army surgeon, John Gordon Smith. In 1828 Smith was appointed England's first professor of forensics, or medical jurisprudence as it was then known, and soon after taking up his post at the University of London, in one of his first lectures Smith disproved Marshall's findings in the Fenning case, and later successfully petitioned the government to make his subject compulsory for all students of medicine. Thererafter the Society of Apothecaries announced a compulsory three-month course in medical jurisprudence for everyone studying for its licence, The Royal College of Surgeons of England and the Royal College of Physicians both following suit. Significant progress indeed; however, in a sad footnote to Eliza Fenning's fate, in 1829, an article was published in the *Morning Journal* detailing the death of Robert Turner, Eliza's employer. Turner had died in an Ipswich workhouse, but before he breathed his last, had confessed himself guilty of the crime for which Fenning had been hanged.

Of course, the scales of justice can weigh either way and it was the outcome of a failed murder trial in 1832, where James Marsh had appeared as the expert witness for the prosecution, which spurred on his efforts to develop a conclusive test for the presence of arsenic. A practical chemist appointed to the Royal Military Academy, Marsh was also an inventor, devoted to metallurgical interests, and it was his knowledge in this field that was instrumental in his development of a reliable method for the detection of arsenic. The test which Marsh developed involved combining a sample containing arsenic with sulphuric acid and arsenic-free zinc; when the resulting arsine gas was ignited, it decomposed to pure metallic arsenic which, when passed over a cold surface, would appear as a silvery-black deposit. So sensitive was the test that it could detect as little as one-fiftieth of a milligram of arsenic, determining whether or not the poison had been a factor in a person's death; certainly enough to convince a doubtful jury. The first publicly documented use of the Marsh Test was in Tulle, France, in 1840 during the infamous case of Madame Marie LaFarge who was found guilty of poisoning her husband. The extensive coverage of the trial in the French press significantly raised the profile and legitimacy of the field of forensic toxicology, and as a consequence of the publicity garnered, the Marsh Test was hailed as a wonder of modern science. The test itself attracted so much interest that for a while it became something of a fairground attraction, with demonstrations conducted in salons, public lectures and even in popular melodramas recreating the LaFarge case.

Though the quality of forensic evidence, and the professional standing of the men who provided it, continued to grow and increasingly contribute to the outcome of a fair, or fairer, trial – in 1841 German chemist Hugo Reinsch published a description of a test which was equally conclusive but was quicker than the Marsh Test – unfortunately the testimony of an expert witness was not necessarily a feature in every poisoning case, as the costs involved were often prohibitively high. Despite the credit due to Dr Addington and James Marsh, it was Alfred Swaine Taylor (1806–1880) a lecturer in forensic toxicology and later chemistry who, during the course of a career that spanned over forty years, contributed immeasurably to the professional establishment of forensic toxicology in England. In bringing scientific evidence into line with the demands of the law with regards to what constitutes proof of poisoning, his textbooks influenced many generations of young scientists, even though Taylor himself was not an outstanding analyst. As Taylor's fame grew, while he was based in London, he was regularly consulted in cases that occurred outside of the capital, even though the services of other capable forensic chemical analysts were available, some of whom had business and academic interests that made them known in other parts of the country. William Herapath (1796–1868), as well as being a political reformer, was one such professional. Mainly associated with cases in the west of England, Herapath had an established reputation, responsible for a first in English forensic analysis when he successfully demonstrated the presence of arsenic in an exhumed corpse buried 14 years previously. Nevertheless, Taylor's services were still eagerly sought and he began to accept samples for analysis from all over the country. And it was Taylor's insistence on receiving a fee that adequately reflected the expenses he incurred that set the standard in charging for such expertise across the board. And the process was not cheap. The meticulous research carried out by Katherine Watson, historian of Forensic Medicine and Crime at Oxford Brookes University, gives an idea of the costs involved. As an example, in 1836 the going rate for analysing the contents of the stomach and intestines was one guinea. However, in practice it was necessary for several different organs and samples to be analysed, so the cost was substantially increased, especially when the reimbursement for man-hours was figured into the equation, six such analyses taking about two days to complete. In addition, there were also the expenses incurred when an analyst consulted with a client, or travelled to give evidence. The potential costs in bringing a poisoning case to trial then were a weighty financial consideration. Consequently, some coroners were hesitant in employing the services of expert witnesses, though more often than not the physician or surgeon carrying out the autopsy won over public opinion of the day.

Returning to Mary Blandy's case, though the substance she administered to her father was doubtless arsenic, we are still left with the quandary as to whether or not she emphatically knew it to be so – the question of her guilt resting on that of her 'intention'. The contemporary opinion would seem to lean toward her being complicit in the crime, though the gossip and hearsay which must have buzzed about the streets of Oxford in April 1752 may well have been inflammatory and misinformed, compounded by the mass of available publications concerning Mary's case. Yet those who might have leafed through a copy of *A Genuine and Impartial Account Of the Life of Miss Mary Blandy*, available from the Oxford bookseller W Jackson in the High Street, priced at 6d, would have read the following passage extolling Mary as an object of 'pity' rather than as an intentional malefactor:

'When we reflect on the Excellence of her natural Qualities and Endowments, improv'd by the best education; when we consider her firm and intrepid Behavior at her Trial; her steady and uniform Seriousness (except in some few Instances) during her Confinement; and her persisting in her Vindication of her Innocence even to her latest Breath at the fatal Tree; all plead strongly in her Favour; and whether really guilty or not, must be left only to the Supreme Judge. To conclude, she was either the most *wicked*, or the most *unfortunate* of Women, but pity and Christian Charity would incline one to believe the latter.'

Yet we might hold Francis Blandy in some part responsible for his daughter's ruination and demise, and in turn his own death; his exaggeration of Mary's dowry certainly directed the events of her life and while doubtless other mountebanks would have been attracted if Cranstoun had not come along, whether they would have resorted to murder is another question. Mr Bathurst, who led for the Crown at Mary's trial, nevertheless excused Francis's deception as 'a pious fraud', warranted in his attempts to attract the 'right' sort of husband for his daughter. Tellingly, even though Cranstoun was financially unprepossessing, with his coveted ties to nobility, in Francis's mind, the captain nevertheless fitted the bill.

Even allowing for a healthy measure of subjective impartiality, it would be easy to cherry-pick the 'facts' as we know them, and to make a case for Mary's guilt, though the assertion of her innocence could equally be upheld if allowances were made for her supposed naiveté. Certainly, the opinion of William Roughead, the well-known Scottish lawyer and amateur criminologist who was an early proponent of the modern 'true crime' literary genre, was clear-cut; Roughead stated in his *Trial of Mary Blandy*, published in 1914, that, 'no one who has studied the evidence against her can entertain a reasonable doubt'. No trace of any forgiving clemency there! But the assumption that Mary acted as a solo criminal, with the cunning to implicate her guileless lover in order to lessen her own guilt must be viewed as preposterous. Yet the question remains; was it possible that Mary was so much in love with Cranstoun that she rationalised away all the 'red flags' fluttering on the breeze of suspicious circumstance leading up to her father's death? The warning signs were there but she did not heed them. Even if instinct and intuition were lacking, surely common sense should have prevailed. In Cranstoun's thrall, was it that Mary was reckless, that she was foolish, or simply besotted to a degree which in hindsight seems absurd? Perhaps she was victim to all of these impulses. It seems incredible, yet even Francis Blandy himself said 'What won't a girl do for a man she loves?'

Certainly, for his part, Cranstoun must be acknowledged as equally culpable at the very least, even if the jury at Mary's trial were of the opinion that his clear involvement did not mitigate her own actions. The numerous references to Cranstoun as a 'villain' would seem to fit the bill. In his criminal intent, a dark picture of the ostensibly charismatic Cranstoun emerges; single-minded, determinedly deceitful and manipulative, with a disregard for the consequences to others, and markedly feeling no remorse for his actions, Cranstoun showed himself as emotionally void, deliberately controlling, with a liberal dash of the compulsive liar thrown into his psychological mix. Yet his charming persona belying his lack of conscience assured that he was well equipped to pursue his avaricious ambition. An ambition sharpened by the lure of Mary's ten thousand pounds, which in today's relative worth would have made him a millionaire – and people have murdered for far less. In engineering the proxy poisoning of Francis by Mary's hand, Cranstoun was cunning enough to afford himself effective deniability; though he could hardly have sent Mary a gift-wrapped dagger with which to stab her father, if she were indeed that controlled by her infatuation to the extent that has been suggested, she may well have gone along with that suggestion if Cranstoun had asked her to!

Whether Mary was an accessory before, or after, the fact, it was the degree of personal treachery which resonated so strongly. There was no room in eighteenth-century society for familial betrayal or fluctuating morals for that matter. It was also to Mary's detriment, and indeed to every other of her sex, that the conviction of women for a serious crime has always attracted, and possibly always will attract, a disproportionate level of attention because of the perceived perversions of 'natural' womanhood that such actions are understood to represent, raising concerns about the perceived role of women, especially within the domestic sphere. Even if Mary's version of the facts were true, she was still guilty of filial disobedience in acquiescing to Cranstoun's attempts to influence her father's sentiments, the criminality of the betrayal of her daughterly duty contextualised by the social and political principles of a society where the concepts of parental, as well as gender respect were firmly entrenched. Masculine authority would have been further affronted by the idea of her inappropriate 'romantic' inclinations, behaviour which placed her in defiance of and outside the bounds of accepted feminine decency. Yet her risk-taking behaviour may have been dictated by those very same accepted notions of femininity with which she was expected to conform – confronted with the contradiction as to whom she regarded her master – whether that was her father or her husband-to-be, clearly the dominance of the latter won through. A supposition supported by a quote from *Cranstoun's Own Version of the Facts*, alleging that Mary had supposedly made a solemn vow that 'no other Man but myself [Cranstoun] should call her Wife... and, she should reckon herself in Duty bound to have the utmost Regard to my Will & Pleasure'. In reality, a 'Will' bent on the 'Pleasure' of attaining Mary's fortune, whatever the cost.

If we accept the commanding role which Cranstoun himself played in the murder of Francis Blandy, it does raise some hypothetical questions, especially if both parties had come to trial together, and even more so, were their cases to be heard in a court of law today. Doubtless, the circumstances would excite a similar frenzy of publicity, the media response equivalent to the level of press attention stirred up in 1752. Pitted against the sophisticated present-day methods of policing and extradition processes, the probability of Cranstoun's apprehension would be significantly increased, the press afforded the opportunity to report on a joint trial. If that trial were to be heard in Oxford again, as an indictable-only case, both Mary and Cranstoun would be brought before the Crown Court, though as a high-profile case, the matter might be referred to the Old Bailey, attracting an even greater deal of publicity.

Following the notional presumption of Cranstoun's appearance in the dock, while there is an element of legal vagueness concerning whether a person instigating a proxy murder is guilty of the crime of murder, the criminal nature of Cranstoun's actions would necessarily be recognised. If he were not charged with the murder itself, Cranstoun might be charged with conspiracy to commit murder and/or being an accessory to murder. With regards to indicting Mary, it is possible that today she might face a lesser charge of constructive manslaughter; the prosecution establishing that she had committed an unlawful act that was dangerous in the sense that a 'reasonable and sober' person would recognise that the act was enough to put the victim at risk of physical harm. Administering poison to a person with criminal intent is in itself a criminal offence, whether actual hurt is caused or not.

Certainly, a modern murder trial would last longer than the thirteen hours in which it took the jury of 1752 to find Mary guilty, and after only five minutes of deliberation without their even retiring from the courtroom. It should be borne in mind however that until 1858 a jury would be kept without fire, food or drink until a verdict was agreed, invariably hastening their decisions. Additionally, in the eighteenth century, prosecutors, judges and even jurors exercised considerable discretion in how they interpreted the law, significantly expediting due process, and in the absence of a fully developed law of evidence, those same prosecutors, judges and jurors had more power and flexibility than they do today. While contemporaries considered past courtroom procedures to be a reasonable means of determining guilt or innocence, from a modern point of view the defence counsel was substantially disadvantaged. Though allowed to call and examine their own witnesses, as well as cross-examine those called by the prosecution, defence counsel were not however permitted to address the jury directly; shifting the burden of proof onto the prosecutor would come later. Thankfully, at variance with those eighteenth century proceedings, once a trial has commenced today, the judge ensures that all parties involved are given the opportunity for their case to be presented and considered as fully and fairly as possible. The contemporary outcome of this 'cold case' then might be very different, especially if Mary's defence counsel cited that their client was the victim of 'ambient abuse'. A form of mental exploitation akin to 'gaslighting', the ambient abuser ostensibly only wants the best for their target. Yet their altruistic behaviour conceals the underlying motive to get the upper hand. If a jury could be persuaded that this form of stealth psychological control was exercised by Cranstoun over Mary, intended to strategically exploit her emotional dependence, and ensuring his dominance and command over her, then the subjective manipulation of Mary into poisoning her father could be viewed as mitigating circumstances in her favour. Certainly, a factor in lessening the severity of her culpability, as she would have been acting under extreme mental and emotional control at the time the crime was committed. If Mary were shown to have been susceptible to, and acting under the influence of such mental exploitation, she might even receive a suspended sentence.

With regards to Cranstoun, while one should never assume how a jury might be swayed, in vindication for his abandonment of Mary, a guilty verdict would seem apposite. To add weight to the charges, the prosecution might even conjecture that Cranstoun's murderous intent was not limited to Francis Blandy alone; he had succeeded in removing the father, why not the daughter? A widower left free to squander his unimaginable wealth, with no limits placed on his dissipation and extravagant expenditure, who knows, perhaps this 'long game' was Cranstoun's objective from the very first, though his defence counsel's likely objection would mean that such a supposition would be struck from the record of proceedings. It is a supposition worthy of consideration nonetheless.

By the prevailing contemporary standards of justice in the eighteenth century, it could be argued that Mary received a fair trial, and her 'coolness' in the face of death, as referenced by Horace Walpole in one of his many letters concerning the Blandy case, has been construed by some as an internal admission of guilt on Mary's part, she feeling that death was a proportional punishment for her crime, or at least for the part she played in her father's death. Yet on reflection, perhaps the temptation to predict a favourable outcome for Mary if she were to stand trial today would be to draw a parallel with the contemporary public sympathy felt for her *after* her execution. In the words of *the Newgate Calendar*, 'the public have ever been divided in opinion on her case'. Yet in spite of the divided opinions with regards to the verdict returned in 1752, the forensic legacy of Mary Blandy's conviction nevertheless cannot be called into question. As a consequence of the initial acceptance of scientific testing in a court of law, the development and contribution of modern forensic understanding is irrefutably a crucial factor in the veracity of the justice served today. But at what price if Mary were indeed innocent? Doubtless the acceptance of and advancements in forensic testing would have been realised at some point, but this is an undeniably contentious issue of historical and indeed moral 'what ifs', especially with regards to the extent that the 'Toxic Truth' played in Mary's conviction. The degree to which the forensic evidence presented in Mary's case influenced and indeed weighed with the consensus of opinion in the matter of her 'intention' in her father's murder is a matter open to conjecture; moreover, how might the verdict have been influenced had Dr Addington's expert evidence been discounted? In turn raising the question, how many other destinies would have been affected by the repercussions of an alternate outcome? Though Francis Blandy's death was doubtless brought about by arsenic poisoning, if Mary was indeed guiltless, and damned for allowing a naiveté nature to dictate her actions, then the true criminality of her case rests in Mary Blandy's wrongful conviction.

Appendix

Bibliography of the Blandy Case, as compiled by Mr Horace Bleackley
(*Some Distinguished Victims of the Scaffold*, 1905)

M ary Blandy's case certainly excited much public opinion, and her trial, conviction and execution proved newsworthy for the best part of 1752, and beyond. Indeed, it was said that 'the pamphleteers kept the discussion alive a year longer than its subject'. In addition to the various verbatim accounts of her trial which appeared in print, Mary was also the subject of numerous publications detailing her life and misdemeanours, not to mention her *Own Account*, a rebuttal to all those slight-worthy publications already in circulation prior to her execution.

Eager to capitalise on the popularity and fascination stirred-up by such high-profile cases, publishers and printers profited from the increasing sales of books, pamphlets and indeed column space devoted to 'heinous' crimes. Apparently shocking the sensibilities of their readers, many were doubtless titillated by the often embellished and lurid details associated with 'celebrity criminals' such as Mary Blandy.

In view of the proliferation of printed matter concerning the Blandy case, it comes as no surprise that when Horace Bleackley came to publish his *Some Distinguished Victims of the Scaffold*, in 1905, included was a diligently compiled bibliography cataloguing no less than thirty references. With the inclusion of 'Contemporary Newspapers and Magazines' in which articles about Mary variously appeared, Bleackley's bibliography is reproduced here in its entirety.

I. Contemporary Tracts

1. *An Authentic Narrative of that most Horrid Parricide*. (Printed in the year 1751. Name of publisher in second edition, M. Cooper.)
2. *A Genuine and full Account of the Parricide* committed by Mary Blandy. Oxford: Printed for and sold by C. Goddard in the High St., and sold by R. Walker in the little Old Bailey, and by all booksellers and pamphlet Shops. (Published 9 November 1751.)

3. *A Letter from a Clergyman to Miss Mary Blandy with her answer thereto.* ...
   As also Miss Blandy's Own Narrative. London; Printed for M. Cooper
   at the Globe in Paternoster Row. 1752. Price Six-pence. Brit. Mus. (20
   March 1752.)

4. *An Answer to Miss Blandy's Narrative.* London; Printed for W. Owen,
   near Temple Bar. 1752. Price 3d. Brit. Mus. (27 March 1752.)

5. *The Case of Miss Blandy considered* as a Daughter, as a Gentlewoman,
   and as a Christian. Oxford; Printed for R. Baldwin, at the Rose in
   Paternoster Row. Brit. Mus. (6 April 1752.)

6. *Original Letters to and from Miss Blandy and C—— C——*, London.
   Printed for S. Johnson, near the Haymarket, Charing Cross. 1752. Brit.
   Mus. (8 April 1752.)

7. *A Genuine and impartial Account of the Life of Miss M. Blandy.* W.
   Jackson and R. Walker. (9 April 1752.)

8. *Miss Mary Blandy's Own Account.* London: Printed for A. Millar in
   the Strand. 1752 (price one shilling and sixpence). N.B. The Original
   Account authenticated by Miss Blandy in a proper manner may be seen
   at the above A. Millar's. Brit. Mus. (10 April 1752. The most famous
   apologia in criminal literature.)

9. *A Candid Appeal to the Public, by a Gentleman of Oxford.* London.
   Printed for J. Clifford in the Old Bailey, and sold at the Pamphleteer
   Shops. 1752. Price 6d. Brit. Mus. (15 April 1752.)

10. *The Tryal of Mary Blandy.* Published by Permission of the Judges.
    London: Printed for John and James Rivington at the Bible and Crown
    and in St. Paul's Churchyard. 1752. In folio price two shillings. 8vo. one
    shilling. Brit. Mus. (24 April 1752.)

11. *The Genuine Histories* of the Life and Transactions of John Swan and
    Eliz Jeffries, ... and Miss Mary Blandy. London: Printed and sold by
    T. Bailey opposite the Pewter-Pot-Inn in Leadenhall Street. (Published
    after 10 April 1752.)

12. *An Authentic and full History of all the Circumstances of the Cruel Poisoning
    of Mr. Francis Blandy*, printed only for Mr. Wm. Owen, Bookseller at
    Temple Bar, London, and R. Goadby in Sherborne. Brit. Mus. (Without
    date. From pp. 113-132 the pamphlet resembles the "Answer to Miss
    Blandy's Narrative," published also by Wm. Owen.)

13. *The Authentic Trials of John Swan and Elizabeth Jeffryes....* With the Tryal
    of Miss Mary Blandy. London: Printed by R. Walker for W. Richards,
    near the East Gate, Oxford. 1752. Brit. Mus. (Published later than the
    "Candid Appeal.")

14. *The Fair Parricide*. A Tragedy in three Acts. Founded on a late melancholy event. London. Printed for T. Waller, opposite Fetter Lane. Fleet Street (price 1/-). Brit. Mus. (5 May 1752.)

15. *The Genuine Speech of the Hon Mr.* ——, at the late trial of Miss Blandy. London: Printed for J. Roberts in Warwick Lane. 1752. (Price sixpence.) Brit. Mus. (15 May 1752.)

16. *The x x x x Packet Broke open*, or a letter from Miss Blandy in the Shades below to Capt. Cranstoun in his exile above. London. Printed for M. Cooper at the Globe in Paternoster Row. 1752. Price 6d. Brit. Mus. (16 May 1752.)

17. *The Secret History of Miss Blandy*. London. Printed for Henry Williams, and sold by the booksellers at the Exchange, in Ludgate St., at Charing Cross, and St. James. Price 1s. 6d. Brit. Mus. (11 June 1752. A sane and well-written account of the whole story.)

18. *Memories of the Life of Wm. Henry Cranstoun, Esqre*. London. Printed for J. Bouquet, at the White Hart, in Paternoster Row. 1752. Price one shilling. Brit. Mus. (18 June 1752.)

19. *The Genuine Lives of Capt. Cranstoun and Miss Mary Blandy*. London. Printed for M. Cooper, Paternoster Row, and C. Sympson at the Bible Warehouse, Chancery Lane. 1753. Price one shilling. Brit. Mus.

20. *Capt. Cranstoun's Account of the Poisoning of the Late Mr. Francis Blandy*. London: Printed for R. Richards, the Corner of Bernard's-Inn, near the Black Swan, Holborn. Brit. Mus. (1-3 March 1753.)

21. *Memories of the life and most remarkable transactions of Capt. William Henry Cranstoun*. Containing an account of his conduct in his younger years. His letter to his wife to persuade her to disown him as her husband. His trial in Scotland, and the Court's decree thereto. His courtship of Miss Blandy; his success therein, and the tragical issue of that affair. His voluntary exile abroad with the several accidents that befel him from his flight to his death. His reconciliation to the Church of Rome, with the Conversation he had with a Rev. Father of the Church at the time of his conversion. His miserable death, and pompous funeral. Printed for M. Cooper in Paternoster Row; W. Reeve in Fleet Street; and C. Sympson in Chancery Lane. Price 6d. With a curious print of Capt. Cranstoun. Brit. Mus. (10-13 March 1753. As the title-page of this pamphlet is torn out of the copy in the Brit. Mus., it is given in full. From pp. 3-21 the tract is identical with "The Genuine Lives," also published by M. Cooper.)

22. *Parricides!* The trial of Philip Stansfield, Gt., for the murder of his father in Scotland, 1688. Also, the trial of Miss Mary Blandy, for the murder of her Father, at Oxford, 1752. London (1810). Printed by J. Dean, 57 Wardour St., Soho for T. Brown, 154 Drury Lane and W. Evans, 14 Market St., St. James's. Brit. Mus.
23. *The Female Parricide*, or the History of Mary-Margaret d'Aubray, Marchioness of Brinvillier.... In which a parallel is drawn between the Marchioness and Miss Blandy. C. Micklewright, Reading. Sold by J. Newbery. Price 1/-. (5 March 1752.)

Lowndes mentions also:—
24. *An Impartial Inquiry into the Case of Miss Blandy*. With reflections on her Trial, Defence, Bepentance, Denial, Death. 1753. 8vo.
25. *The Female Parricide*. A Tragedy, by Edward Crane, of Manchester. 1761. 8vo.
26. *A Letter from a Gentleman to Miss Blandy* with her answer thereto. 1752. 8vo. (Possibly the same as "A Letter from a Clergyman.")

The two following are advertised in the newspapers of the day:—
27. *Case of Miss Blandy and Miss Jeffries* fairly stated, and compared.... R. Robinson, Golden Lion, Ludgate Street. (26 March 1752.)
28. *Genuine Letters between Miss Blandy and Miss Jeffries* before and after their Conviction. J. Scott, Exchange Alley; W. Owen, Temple Bar; G. Woodfall, Charing Cross. (21 April 1752.)
29. Broadside. *Execution of Miss Blandy*. Pitts, Printer, Toy and Marble Warehouse, 6 Great St. Andrew's St., Seven Dials. Brit. Mus.
30. *The Addl. MSS.*, 15930. Manuscript Department in the Brit. Mus.

II. Contemporary Newspapers and Magazines

1. *Read's Weekly Journal*, March and April (1752), 3 February (1753).
2. *The General Advertiser*, August–November (1751), March and April (1752).
3. *The London Evening Post*, March and April (1752).
4. *The Covent Garden Journal* (Sir Alexander Drawcansir), February, March, and April (1752).
5. *The London Morning Penny Post*, August and September (1751).
6. *Gentleman's Magazine*, pp. 396, 486–88 (1751), pp. 108–17, 152, 188, 195 (1752), pp. 47, 151 (1753), p. 803, pt. II (1783).
7. *Universal Magazine*, pp 114–124, 187, 281 (1752).

8. *London Magazine*, pp. 379, 475, 512 (1751), pp. 127, 180, 189 (1752), p. 89 (1753).

[In addition to the two London editions of the authorised report of the trial specified in No. 10 of the Bibliography, it may be noted that the trial was reprinted at length in the same year at Dublin, and in an abridged form at London and Edinburgh, all 8vo.—ED.]

Bibliography

N.B. To avoid repetition, the contemporary publications referenced throughout the text are listed amongst the bibliography compiled by Horace Bleackley in the Appendix.

AINSWORTH MITCHELL, C., *A Scientist in the Criminal Courts*, Chapman & Hall, London, 1945.

AINSWORTH MITCHELL, C., *Science and the Criminal*, Little, Brown & Company, Boston, 1911.

BEATTIE, John M., *The Criminality of Women in Eighteenth-century England*, Journal of Social History, 1975.

BLEACKLEY, Horace, *Some Distinguished Victims of the Scaffold*, (1905), The Project Gutenberg, 2016.

CHRISTISON, Robert, *A Treatise on Poisons: In Relation to Medical Jurisprudence, Physiology, and the Practice of Physic*, Black, Edinburgh, 1829

CLARKE, Michael, CRAWFORD, Catherine, *Legal Medicine in History*, Cambridge University Press, 1994.

CULLEN, William R., *Is Arsenic an Aphrodisiac?: The Sociochemistry of an Element*, Royal Society of Chemistry, London, 2008.

DAVIES, Owen, *Popular Magic: Cunning-folk in English History*, Hambledon Continuum, London, 2007.

DUBBER Markus D., and FARMER, Lindsay, (Editors), *Modern Histories of Crime and Punishment*, Stanford University Press, California, 2007.

DURSTON, Gregory J., *Wicked Ladies: Provincial Women, Crime and the Eighteenth-Century English Justice System*, Cambridge Scholars Publishing, Newcastle upon Tyne, 2014.

EMSLEY, John, *The Elements of Murder: A History of Poison*, Oxford University Press, Oxford, New York, 2005.

FARRELL, Michael, *Criminology of Homicidal Poisoning: Offenders, Victims and Detection*, Springer, New York, 2017.

GOLAN, T, *Laws of men and laws of nature: the history of scientific expert testimony in England and America*, Harvard University Press, Cambridge, MA, and London, 2004.

HEINZELMAN, Susan, *Representing Women: Law, Literature, and Feminism*, Duke University Press, North Carolina, 1994.

HEINZELMAN, Susan, *Riding the Black Ram: Law, Literature, and Gender*, Stanford University Press, California, 2010.

HEMPEL, Sandra, *The Inheritor's Powder: A Tale of Arsenic, Murder, and the New Forensic Science*, W. W. Norton & Company, New York, 2013.

HILL, Bridget, *Women, Work & Sexual Politics in Eighteenth-century England*, McGill-Queen's University Press, Ontario 1994.

HOOPER, Mary, *Newes from the Dead*, Random House, London, 2012.

LANDAU, Norma, *Gauging Crime in Late Eighteenth-Century London*, Social History 35, 2010.

LONGMAN, HURST, REES, ORME and BROWN, *A Complete Collection of State Trials and Proceedings for High Treason and Other Crimes and Misdemeanors from the Earliest Period to the Year 1783, with Notes and Other Illustrations, Volume 2*, London 1816.

LOWNDES, William Thomas, *The Bibliographer's Manual of English Literature: containing an account of rare, curious, and useful books, published in or relating to Great Britain and Ireland*, Bell & Daldy, London, 1869.

MCLYNN, Frank, *Crime and Punishment in Eighteenth-century England*, Routledge, New York, 1989.

PEARSE, Bowen, *Ghost-Hunter's Casebook*, The History Press, Stroud, Gloucestershire, 2007.

ROUGHEAD, William, Editor, *Trial of Mary Blandy*, (1914), The Project Gutenberg, 2004.

SAXTON, Kirsten T., *Narratives of Women and Murder in England, 1680-1760: Deadly Plots*, Ashgate Publishing Ltd, Farnham, Surrey, 2009.

SEILER, Hans G., (Editor), SIGEL, A., SIGEL, H., *Handbook on Metals in Clinical and Analytical Chemistry*, Marcel Dekker, New York, 1994.

STRATMANN, Linda, *The Secret Poisoner: A Century of Murder*, Yale University Press, London, 2016.

STREIKER, Carol S., and **STREIKER, Jordan M.**, *The Seduction of Innocence: The Attraction And Limitations Of The Focus On Innocence In Capital Punishment Law And Advocacy*, Journal Of Criminal Law & Criminology, 2005.

WARD, Richard M., *Print Culture, Crime and Justice in 18th-Century London*, Bloomsbury Publishing, London, 2014.

WATSON, Katherine D., *Forensic Medicine in Western Society: A History*, Routledge, Abingdon-on-Thames, 2010.

WATSON, Katherine D., *Medical and Chemical Expertise in English Trials for Criminal Poisoning, 1750–1914*, US National Library of Medicine, 2006.

WATSON, Katherine D., *Poisoned Lives: English Poisoners and Their Victims*, Hambledon Continuum, London, 2004.

WEXLER, Dr Philip, *History of Toxicology and Environmental Health: Toxicology in Antiquity, Volumes I & II*, Academic Press, London, 2014.

WHORTON, James C., *The Arsenic Century: How Victorian Britain was Poisoned at Home, Work and Play*, Oxford University Press, Oxford, 2010.

WYNDHAM, Horace, *The Mayfair Calendar - Some Society Causes Célèbres*, Hutchinson & Co Ltd, London, 1926.

Additional Sources
Cracroft's Peerage, The Complete Guide to the British Peerage & Baronetage
The London Magazine: Or, Gentleman's Monthly Intelligencer, (*The Gentleman's Magazine*), 1752.
MeasuringWorth.com, Purchasing Power of British Pounds from 1270 to Present.
Murder Act (1752), London: HMSO. (25 Geo 2 11, c 37)
The Newgate Calendar at the Ex-classics website.

Index